I Remember Flowers

A book of poetry by
Karen Melander Magoon

Books by Karen Melander Magoon

Scores: Lillie, A Musical; Georgia, Musical Portrait of the Artist, Georgia O'Keeffe; Clara, Angel of the Battlefield, Musical Portrait of Clara Barton
Books of Poetry: A Year of Anguish, A Time for Miracles; The Earth Turns
Various Anthologies and Publications

Copyright © 2021 by Curious Muse

All rights reserved. No part of this book may be reproduced by any means, including information storage and retrieval or photocopying, except for short excerpts in critical articles, without written permission of the publisher.

ISBN- 978-1-7355892-3-7

Curious Muse Press
San Francisco

Preface

"I Remember Flowers" echoes from my childhood, my adolescence, the gardens I nurtured in my adulthood and now, walking in gardens, the surprise of a sudden pungent aroma of jasmine, the sight of a rosebud beginning to open, or a hummingbird tucking into violet exuberance.

"I Remember Flowers" is also a recognition of indigenous peoples who have courageously protected their land and waters, the flowers and lakes of ancient times, their heritage and the gardens of earth. It is a recognition of our responsibility to earth and all living things; our responsibility to our rivers and oceans that sustain us, to keep them clean and rid them of plastics and contaminants; and our responsibility to our fellow human beings, the children and the vulnerable, that everyone may have a place in the sun, a place with flowers.

"I Remember Flowers" recognizes all that have gone before that we must remember and honor: ancient kingdoms and peoples, bygone civilizations upon which we have built our own cities and societies; those we have nurtured as well as those we have exploited; lost eras and ages we try to understand as well as our modern era, fraught with pandemic, protests and sometimes overlooked possibilities.

As with all of my books and music, "I Remember Flowers" is a pastiche of thoughts and ideas conveyed through poetry. It is an attempt to hold up a mirror that reflects who we are today and lets us see the ludicrous and the lovely, the foolish and the wise, the pain and the potential for healing.

TABLE OF CONTENTS

I Remember Flowers	10
Western Sahara	12
A Gray Day at the Shoreline	14
We Are Ancestors	15
Last night the Gibbous Moon	16
Chocolate Slavery	17
Breaking the Mirror	19
Indigenous Dance during Corona	20
Seek the Open Door	21
Bathing Persephone	22
Lesotho	23
Building Socialism on Covid	25
I Can't Breathe	26
Pier 4 Burned	28
Monday Rains	29
Venezuela Elections	30
Nine More Shopping Days	31
Pursuit	32
A Boy Story	33
A Dappled Sky	35
Mavi Marmara Tragedy	36
Nakba Continues	37
Devastation and Prayers	38
Seeds	40
A Story from Costa Rica	42
Pearly Rain	44
Deb Haaland for the Interior	45
Blackhole	46
Shooting Stars	48
For the Sake of the Baby in the Manger	50
I am Oromo	51
Democracy is Dying	53
You are more than you	55
Reaching into Fog	57
Congress on the Bay	59
Alcatraz	61
Dreams and Glass	62
A Damp Dawn	64
Lashes in Saudi Arabia, Amnesty International	65
Anti-bias Training at Wiesenthal Center	67
Gillnets and Mercury	69
Summer Scene	71
Ozon	73
Within a Flower	74

Somalia	76
The Sight of the Child	79
Waiting for the Storm	80
Rain Continues	81
100 000 Poets for Change	82
The Year Rolls Out	85
Scenes on a Rainy Night	87
Conjunction of Jupiter and Saturn	90
Christmas Tree in Beirut	92
I Walk Through the Garden	94
Northern Spool	96
Global Events	97
A Christmas Star	98
Journalists Killed	100
Legend of Mount Kelimutu	103
Mongolia	105
Coins	107
Christmas Scene	108
Finding Vision	109
Going to Mars	111
Pomegranate	113
Light on the Ganges	114
Pain	115
My Journey	117
Halos on a City	119
The Cold Wolf Moon	120
Blessing	121
Gratitude and Awe	122
Visiting Golden Gate Park	124
No Space for Grief	125
Less or More	127
A Tiny Story	129
Marguerite	130
A Door	131
Love	132
New Year 2021	133
Arm of Fog	135
Kashmir	136
Sri Lanka	139
Mindanao Durian Fruit	141
South Sudan	143
Sumatra	145
Today I Wept	149
A Chill	151
Aleph	152
Sweeping the Halls of Congress	154
Rocks	156

Someone said to me	157
Cleaning Up	158
Cave Son Doong	159
A Frigid Cave	161
…and they'll come home…	162
Cracks, Rags and Watercolors	163
Metal Detectors for Legislators	164
Baby Megnetar	165
A Small Red House	167
Light whispering	169
Metamorphous of Cloud	170
Finding Tomorrow	171
Not yet Finished Moon	172
Petra	173
Jehudah Halevi	175
Odyssey of Carmenere	178
Together	182
Algeria	184
Pain and Kindness	188
Natural Friend	190
Rainbow Diva	191
A Moon Moment	192
An Unacknowledged Miracle	193
Navalny Waits	194
Awakening	196
I Walk with Shadows	197
Another Day	198
The Rugged Road to Hana	200
I am Sure	201
Love and Nature	202
Rock of our Nation	203
Wings to Forever	204
Only Questions	205
Spring Survives	206
Morning Moon	207
Shadowless	208
Home in a Closed World	209
Nevermore	211
Let us Name the Names	212
Fame	215
The Iron Road	217
The Moon was Hiding	221
Knowing Where You Are	222
Cyrus the Great of Persia	223
Prison to Punish	225
Regard!	229
Tikkun	231

Ides	232
Her Hair	233
The Fog Settles	234
As I Child I Walked	235
Autumn Scene	236
Billy Goats	237
Yesterday a Cat	238
Wild Boar at Five O'clock	239
The Bay Window	240
Green Parrots Congregate	241
A Tiny Bird	242
Deep Red Roses	243
Early Sun	244
A Dog	245
Soft Twilight	246
Impossibly Stretched Cat	247
Wisdom of Life	248
Something Scary	250
On the Yangtze	251
Shadows of Clouds	252
Accepting the Sun	254
Today the Clouds	256
Cat's Tail	257
Twilight in the Rain	258
Closet Door	259
Willow	260
Care	261
Buds	262
Wrinkles	263
Waiting Clouds	264
Stripes	265
Eve II	266
AMELIA	284
If There Were Peace	290
May All of us find Love	291
Song for the Persian New Year	292
Last Night the Moon`	293
My Hummingbird, A Hummingbird Spins	294
Autumn Etchings	295
Morning endeavor	296
The Moon a Cross	297
Kwan Yen to Repair	298
Evening Sky and Rapunzel	299
My Daughter and a Pug	300
The Land Suffers	303
Life Comes Full Circle	305
Jaqueline Makes Soufflés	306

Chrissy Field Fleet Week	307
Coit Tower a Pumpkin	309
La Jolla Cove	310
October Ran	311
October Trees	312
The Voyeurs' Eyes	313
A Universe of Silence	314
Lethal Dragonflies	315
Trophies	317
Detritus of Life and Dreams	318
I Walk Through the Garden, SF Ferry Building	319
To Be a Martyr or Survive	
9,000 Butterflies	320
A Headache	321
People in Portland	322
December 12/12/12	323
Politics and Dreams	324
Flag in the Rain	327
Each Day the Sky Dances	328
People Kill	329
Homeless Dilemma	330
The Aftermath of Bin Laden	332
Sandy Struck	333
Jesus Born in Palestine	334
Sleep and Children	335
The Year has Begun	337
The Common Cold	338
Dark Clouds at Dawn	339
Terror Walks the Streets	340
My Leaf	341
Sublime of Mundane	342

I Remember Flowers

I remember flowers
Or rather
I remember tasting their nectar
Not knowing they were nasturtiums
I remember walking along sidewalks
On my way to school
Stopping to pick the flowers
All different colors
And taste their sweetness
I remember the sidewalk shaking
From an earthquake
I was seven
And lived in Seattle
And walked everywhere alone
It seemed okay then
To walk everywhere alone
I visited the man across the street
Who gave me magazines about Arabian horses
And the woman next door
Who gave me fresh Swedish curly crisp flat bread
I don't know what it was
But it was Swedish so it was good
Because I was Swedish
And lots of other things
I tried to write them all down in school
And the teacher stopped me
And said I was American
And I said no, I was Scotch-Irish, Dutch, Welsh,
French, English, German and half Swedish
I did not write American
I remember going to Woodland Park

To take the ponies around ten times
To earn one ride
I thought Woodland Park was close
Until I visited many years later
I must have walked far by myself
To get to Woodland Park
Later I rode my bicycle
To go to the library
I left it outside unlocked
I said someone might need it
One day the bicycle was gone
I said it's okay
Someone needed it
It will come back
So I read more books
Until the bicycle came back
And I rode home
With books in my basket

Western Sahara

The world forgets

The Sahrawi are a people

Living in their own country

Western Sahara

The world forgets

Eighty countries recognize their independence

Their right to their home

Once nomadic tribes and the Tuareg

Settled and farmed their land

Lived off its fish and crops

In happiness and justice

Until foreign countries coveted its oil and minerals

Until foreign countries decided to steal its wealth

The world forgets

Morocco has no right to Sahrawi land

And yet steals its wealth

Occupies and settles its land

Fishes its waters

Contrary to international law

Contrary to the will of the Sahrawi

While the United States gives its blessing

The world forgets

Violence against vulnerable countries

Is wrong and illegal

Forgets to condemn

Aerial bombardment of napalm and white phosphorus

On Sahrawi refugee camps

Some fleeing to Algeria or Mauritania

Which also wants to bite into the delicious

Western Sahara apple

Polisario students from the university

Fight for the Sahrawi

While Morocco builds a sand berm

Slicing through Western Sahara

To protect the riches of the Sahrawi for themselves

Israel and the United States

Give away something they have no right to

Give away Western Sahara to Morocco

To further steal its treasures

As once Spain and France

Siphoned off its phosphate

Stole its minerals and land

Fished its waters

Forgetting

The Sahrawi are a people

The Sahrawi have a right

To their own land

Forgetting

Because it is convenient to forget

Justice and law

A Gray Day at the Shoreline

A silver knife lies upon the horizon

Sharply cutting into soft mist

Large birds sweep across the sky

Pulling grey rainclouds

In their wake

A small girl does cartwheels

Across the sand to the shore

Memories tumble among the waves

And tear against suddenly slicing rain

We Are Ancestors

We are ancestors

Of those not yet born

We are memories

For those we may

Never know

We gather flowers

Whose seeds and roots

Smile at those

Long past

Long to come

We see cloud formations

Unique yet still familiar

To those who dreamt

For those who loved

Under their softness

Years ago

We see sunsets

And a borealis sky

Never before seen

Yet repeated in a million variations

For those we love

As in the beating of our hearts

Today tomorrow yesterday

In timelessness of time

Last Night the Gibbous Moon

Last night the gibbous moon was melting gold on the horizon
The sky empty of stars yet hanging in folds of velvet over the mountains
Wishes slid covertly through rags of cloud floating anonymously across the night
Nameless bits of cotton ignorant of their purpose
Sat upon the velvet of the sky as I child might paste them upon cardboard
Imagining she made white sheep march across a cardboard sky
Pretending that their journey over starless hills
Could wish the night sky into day

Chocolate Slavery

The moon has risen here

From its cradle behind the horizon

In Africa where a bright sun rises in the east

The moon saw two million children

Bedded down after a long day harvesting chocolate

For Hershey, Mars, Nestle, Cargill

And now leaves Africa to rise on our night sky

While two million young Africans stretch into the sun

To start another day putting cocoa in baskets

For corporations that live off of their arms and legs

Corporations that make it impossible for these small laborers

To go to school

To play as children

To learn about their Africa

To read and write

To climb trees and laugh with their friends

In a paradise for everyone

The children instead exhaust their bodies every day

For chocolate

For our Hershey bars, our luxurious Lady Godiva truffles

The chocolate on our ice cream bars

The chocolate of our Santa Claus and Easter Bunny morsels

Our own congress says it's fine

The law from 1789

Called the Alien Tort

Made it illegal for corporations to abuse human rights abroad

Illegal to detain children for work

But the law has been ignored

Children do not have strong voices

Corporations exercise the power of money and influence

And soon will see injustice come to roost in our country too

For those who have no voice

Who have no power

Like the little ones in Africa

Who only sleep under the moon

And wake to the hot sun

To follow its track through the sky

As their small hands pull and gather

Cocoa for our chocolate

Breaking the Mirror

Dark state
Dark side of truth
Hidden covert
Journalists killed
Truth killed
But never dead
Where is justice
For those who speak truth
Assange Snowden Manning
Where is justice
Who will speak for truth
Who will speak truth
Who are we as a people
As individuals
Who are we
Who cannot look truth in the face
Without breaking the mirror

Indigenous Dance during Corona

Coronavirus struck the indigenous
Secoya nation of 700 people
All with the last name Payguaie
In the Ecuadorian Amazon in April
Indigenous people in Brazil, Peru, and beyond
Die of Coronavirus in the midst of oil fields and palm trees
Where they are forced to work
To mine for oil and harvest palm
Fearing the death of their culture
As their elders die one by one
Knowing the loss of even one elder
Means a push towards extinction
Loss of culture of language of history
By November 3000 cases and 700 deaths
Morgues overflowing
People ask to quarantine
But must work in the rainforest
To mine and drill for oil
In the midst of a pandemic
Tribal chiefs now gather their tribes
Gather their children to dance at each death
To sing at each death
To speak their language at each death
That their cultures may not die

Seek the Open Door

Energy and love is everywhere

Energy and love

Everywhere

In everyone

In everything

Seek the energy

Seek the love

Seek the open door

Walk into energy

Walk into love

As flowers seek cracks to emerge

As waters flow around and over obstacles

As sound finds its echo in canyons

Canyons dug out by water seeking outlet

Wearing away at stony arms

Embracing its surge

Walk into love until the energy opens all doors

Until the energy of love

Bathes all the earth

Embraces the earth

Opens the doors of our hearts

To everyone

To everything

Everywhere

Bathing Persephone

The grasses bleed into the spring
And yet they are born of eternity
They fear the awakening
The pregnancy of their greening
Their thin, eternal roots hesitate
As they push downwards and upwards
Knowing it is their destiny to push
They are the veins of the earth
Pulsing with the blood of creation
Breathing with the lungs of Gaia
Embracing Demeter's Persephone
Still sleeping under the River Styx
Waiting to return to the maidens of the fields
Waiting to dance with garlands of joy
While the grasses hesitate
Demeter prepares a celebration
As the soul of earth dreams
Dreams dreams of dancing
Dreams dreams of nectar
Filling the goblets of rebirth
Demeter pours nectar out on all the world
The wine of the gods
That Persephone may bathe
In its redemption

Lesotho

Moshaishai was born into kingship of Lesotho
As was Shaka Zulu born to be king of Zulu in South Africa
Moshaishai believed power comes from the people
And from generosity to one's opponents
Led his troops to the top of the mountain
To protect his country against the current wars
Of South Africa
To protect his people against apartheid
To protect Lesotho from falling into
South African hands
Or the military might of Shaka Zulu
As a Bantustan
A small kingdom
40,000 years old
Lesotho has mineral wealth
And rivers and mountains
Enough water in water starved southern Africa
Yet is landlocked
It is a monarchial democracy
Enjoying a succession of benign rulers
Moshaishai I left a legacy of peace
Through negotiation and skill
When the Boers stole his country's cattle
He told them to keep it and cease warring

They agreed, but fought again
So he took back his cattle through military cunning
Yet asked Britain to protect his little country
Disputes about borders continued
But the people of Lesotho thrived
Moshaishai left an example of winning battles
But giving land to his enemies
Rather than exacting retribution
Shaka Zulu, his opposition, mentally ill
Was assassinated by his half-brothers
But Moshaishaie was beloved because he listened to his people
Because he knew the people and their congress
Did not want to be ruled by South Africa
Yet did not want war
And taught his sons to rule well
To work with congress
To be friends with neighbor nations
A poor but proud people
Whose rulers believe in democracy
And self-government
And the bargaining power
Of negotiation and generosity
And rule by consensus
The kingdom of Lesotho
And its benign rulers should be a mentor
For the world

Building Socialism on Covid

Building socialism on the backs of Covid
On the backs of the elephant in the room
Showing himself with faces on zoom
Wondering if he's really Republican too
But merely escaped from a city zoo
A ghost in distress curious what will come next
As the world hunkers down and has no rest
Till a vaccine arrives like a shiny white knight
To rescue us all, to save all in sight
The elephant conjures and curls his trunk
Sitting down in the corner and waiting for Trump
To get out of sight to leave the scene
With pockets of hydroxychloroquine
The elephant waits in a room become small
As the whole world awaits his beck and call
Bernie Sanders had hoped for a socialist state
Health care for all, the homeless can't wait
For homes and protection for medicine too
But the elephant wants to go back to the zoo

I Can't Breathe

Eric Garner
Now George Floyd
How many others
Have died through police choking
Is police murder
Still sanctioned?
Will we have no trust left
For police who shoot and choke
For the crime of being black?
Will no one want to join the ranks
Of the police ever again
To protect and assist
As is the purpose of police
How many times have police murdered?
How many tunes will police murder again?
How many times have they heard
I can't breathe
And let their victims suffocate
With impunity?
Michigan's capitol is stormed
Racists with nooses, long rifles
Confederate flags
Protest lockdown
While in that same state

Black men are killed by police

For petty unproven crimes

The white mob storms the capitol

With impunity

Injustice reigns

On the Michigan streets

Where police become thugs

And history repeats

Pier 45 Burned, May 24, 2020, San Francisco

Pier 45 burned on Saturday

Emptying out a warehouse of crab cages

And homeless

No one died

Though many lost their life work

Years of gathered fishing supplies

But the smoldering continued

Continued through Memorial weekend

Continued Monday and Tuesday

Creosote burns and smokes

Smolders and chokes

Fossil fuels, oil and tar

Slapped on wood to preserve it

When burnt

Sends fumes into the sky

Carcinogens and asthma inducing fumes

Coal leaves its calling card everywhere

Even when it is destroyed and destroying

It remains an unwelcome

But memorable guest

Monday Rains

It seems the world is bathed this morning
As rain pours down the streets and windows
Washing the city in freshness
Giving the lemon trees and hibernating flowers
A welcome drink after parched months
Pouring down below the roots of giant trees
To soak the earth in moisture

Venezuela Elections December 2020

Venezuela breathes easy

Venezuela votes

Venezuela affirms

The wish of the people

Venezuela says no to oligarchy

No to foreign capitalism

No to the thumb of the west

Venezuela votes freedom

For the party of the late Chavez

Venezuela affirms its control

Of its own resources

Venezuela affirms the will

Of the people

We approach a new era

We approach an era

Of the people

And pray

All will be well

Nine More Shopping Days

Nine more shopping days before Christmas
And many more die of Covid
Or are hospitalized
While a two year old child
Is abandoned at Goodwill
With a note and a sack of clothes
And Mr. and Mrs. Santa Claus
Test positive for the virus
While children wish for toys for Christmas
Not a virus wrapped in a white beard
Nine more shopping days before Christmas
While 337 Nigerian boys remain kidnapped
After their school was attacked by Boko Haram
Dedicated to abolishing education and knowledge
Adding 337 more to the 10,000 boys
It has kidnapped in the last three years
Some as young as five
Nine more shopping days before Christmas
While we celebrate Beethoven's birthday
Beethoven who wrote "All men shall be brothers"
Beethoven who proclaimed peace in his Ninth Symphony
Nine more shopping days before Christmas
While we pray for peace and love
And for the children

Pursuit

The chickadee is a sweet little bird
Thought he'd found his true love with a call, with a word
But he did not pursue her, too proud and too shy
Now they both are alone in one tree, in one sky
Then our chickadee did find a sweet little finch
And he sought out his friendship you see, inch by inch
But his finch found a girl with a quite different hue
A little brown finch he would like to pursue
She yielded at last to his amorous quest
Now they talk to their young in a sweet little nest
While the chickadee and his would be bride
Remain quite alone in their tree in their sky
Except for those moments when the finch leave their bower
To join with our chickadee for happy hour

A Boy Story

A chickadee whistles
The bay window shines
A boy looks out on Chestnut
As the sun declines
His palace an old bed
Under the panes
Of his window on Mason
Where he alone reigns
It's his San Francisco
He discovered himself
And will always return
Like a book to its shelf
The moon looked in briefly
A new moon last night
A crescent to dream on
A sliver of light
At three in the morning
The boy raises his head
He's not home, he's at Tutu's
But safe in his bed
He remembers tomorrow
He'll visit the park
Do whatever he wants
Now he'll sleep, it's still dark

Back at home, back in Portland

His socks dream of him

And his cables and clutter

Bits of childhood grow dim

But they're all there to welcome him

With flowers in full bloom

When he's flown back to Portland

And back in his room

A Dappled Sky

A dappled sky looks down bemused
Gathering its silken skirts touched with light
Still and unmoving
As the wind gathers beneath
On city streets and trees
Petals of cherry blossoms scatter
Reminders of rosy glory
Yet the petals remain
A carpet for empty streets
Quiet, serene, peaceful
One blue glove sits in a gutter
While a broken white and blue mask
Sits bedraggled on the pavement
Waiting for nothing
Anticipating nothing
Under a dappled sky

Mavi Marmara Tragedy

Twenty years ago Mavi Marmara
On a humanitarian mission
In international waters
With other ships
Part of its fleet
With medicine and medical assistance
To help the victims of Israeli brutality in Gaza
Nearly at its destination
Mavi Marmara, a Turkish ship
Carrying dedicated persons from many different countries
With a single compassionate goal
Was attacked and nine killed
Later a tenth died of his wounds
Blood covered the deck of the Mavi Marmara
And tears from an old man wanting to go home
After years in exile from his beloved Palestine
Yet Gaza remains the densest prison in the world
Under hostile occupation by Israel
Who kill even those attempting to help
Traveling in international waters
Who have done little to aid their Palestinian prisoners
In time of Covid
Save for allowing them to convert factories to make masks
And protective gear for buyers in Asia

Nakba Continues

Al Aqsa spreads her arms
To welcome those who worship
Yet Israel emptied her arms on Friday
Abolishing worship
A further affront to those under her shadow
Ubai Aboudi, American citizen and leading scientist
Imprisoned two months before a conference he led
Took place in January
Still imprisoned and tortured
Awaiting trial without due process
Before a military court
For trumped up charges
With him nearly 5,000 political prisoners
And countless children languish in Israeli prisons
Where Coronavirus lurks
And prisoners are not safe
Nearly four billion dollars in aid
Goes to Israel from the USA
Yet Aboudi, American citizen
And thousands of other political prisoners
Along with children taken from their homes
At dead of night
Remain imprisoned
And ignored by our government

Devastation and Prayers

I am Amphan

I am a cyclone

I rip into people's homes

People in tents

People who have nothing

And I take the nothing they have

I am Amphan

My name means sky

Umpun they say

I rip across Bengal

Where tiny tidepools make playgrounds

For children and small things

I cannot help the force I bring

My throat bellows

I pour floods of water on tiny things

I wipe out life

Like giving birth

Nature pushes my belly

And wind and water surge and destroy

Mother of wind and water and all life

Blows viruses and microbes

Tinier than even I imagine

Into these same tents I now destroy

I blow and scream

Ruled by my mother

I cannot stop my wind and water

I swallow up roofs and bridges

I drink villages and spit them out

And when it is over

I am still Amphan

I am sky

My clouds gather

And I pray

For the world

Beneath me

Seeds

I picked up some shells
And soft abandoned moist tendrils
Under an enormous eucalyptus
Stretching huge limbs out
Over the Fort Mason meadow
And garden
And then put them back
Perhaps a hermit thrush
Or a sparrow
Might enjoy the yearning seeds
Or perhaps
They will find their way
Underground
To wiggle into moisture and humus
Push roots into the earth
And sprout incipient Eucalyptus
Conceived in dark soils
Embraced by giant mother roots
Firmly supporting a scaling trunk
Home to woodpeckers
Home to insects and squirrels
Home to vibrations and scents of life
Mother to small seeds tumbled beneath her limbs
Mother to nascent sprouts

Soon to greet the springtime

To be nursed by the sun and wind and rain

And wonder in awe

At her mother reaching far above

Over the meadow

Over her children

Pushing sprouts

Into an embracing world

A Story from Costa Rica

There was once a beautiful witch named Zarate

Living in the town of Aserri in Costa Rica

On top of a cliff

Who loved the handsome governor

But whose love was not reciprocated

So, being a witch

She turned him into a peacock

And all the townspeople into forest animals

And the city into an enormous rock

The broken heart of a witch

Soon many people came to settle again in Aserri

Not knowing of the witch

Who lived inside her broken heart

With her peacock on a golden chain

Who could be a man again

If he would consent to

Be her husband

Every night she opened her enormous heart

To all the forest creatures

To find food and shelter

One day a poor widower

With many children

Decided to walk up the cliff to Aserri

To ask her help

He was very tired and slept by the rock
When he woke two doves told him to knock three times
And the beautiful witch Zarate would answer
So he knocked and asked courteously
If the beautiful witch would come out
So she came out with her peacock on a chain
And heard his story
His wife had gone swimming in the mountains
And never returned
The witch gave him grapefruits to take to his children
And twelve doves to lead him home
He dropped the grapefruits off the cliff
Too tired to carry them further
And came home to his children
The next day his wife came riding home on a horse
And the children gathered the grapefruits
Which had turned to gold
And thanked the witch Zarate
Who lived inside her broken heart
With her peacock
Her dream of requited love
Never to be realized
As witches, we know,
Are just dreams of magic
Available to anyone
Who will climb the mountain

Pearly Rain

The rain falls inside out on the window
Showing her pearly undergarments
Decorating the wings of birds
Wishing themselves into the arms of spring
Singing secret songs to the wind
Weeping tears of happiness
While the sun dances on pearls
Slipping out of her bright shell
Onto a damp and waiting city

Deb Haaland for the Interior

She says she will be fierce

Fighting for underserved communities

Fighting for our environment

Fighting against expansion of fossil fuels

Fighting for indigenous land

Fighting for sacred lakes and rivers and forests

She was born in Arizona

Her mom is a Laguna Pueblo native

Her father a Marine

As a Marine brat she bounced

Between 13 public schools at military bases

At 15 she worked at a bakery

Food stamps helped her through law school

Homelessness helped her understand life

After one term fighting for New Mexico in Congress

Haaland now hopes to lead the Interior Department

Managing one-fifth of the land in the US

She says she will be fierce

Fighting for the people, the land

And for the sacred trust of indigenous peoples

For all people of the soil and sea and mountains

And the planet we all inhabit

Blackhole

When a star implodes

And becomes a black hole

It disappears

But where does it go?

The shadow of a sphere

The luminous halo around the black hole

Casts a shadow

Like the rings encircling Saturn

When two black holes merge

The event horizons bubble into audible ringing

Deformation and growth

Settles into flawlessness

All black holes are similar

Some larger or smaller but perfect

When they merge they become one again

None created through light

But through music

Through the bell of the universe

All blackholes are perfectly identical

Should debris enter a blackhole

It also implodes in ringing

And then disappears

And the blackhole remains as it was

Featureless informationless

Impossible to decipher

A perfect empty place

A ghost

Or the smile of a Cheshire Cat

After the cat has disappeared

Accompanied by the ringing of the universe

Like a giant cat's bell

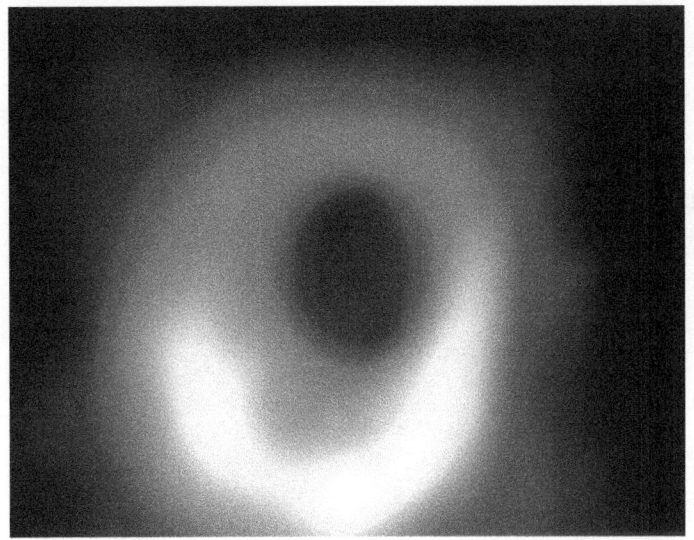

Shooting Stars

How do we quantify gravity?

Does a shooting star demonstrate gravity

Do stars evaporate through a quantum process

Taking them through the other side of the mirror

Humming black holes

Discard quantum bits

Into emptiness that is yet capable

Of stealing energy

From the vacuum

Created by bubbling collision of holes

Into an empty region of space

What it absorbs remains

Like the snuffing out of the light of a candle

Lost in space

And yet no more capable of disappearing

Than exploding bubbles

Or melted ice

Every galaxy is sculpted by a black hole

Residing in its center

Infinitely heavier than its galaxy

Shooting stars land and divide

In the cusp of a black hole

Providing a disk to slide out of its own event

Entangled pairs cancel each other

Yet do not manifest concretely
Wormholes connect particles
Stolen by black holes from the vacuum
Flying through entangled wormholes like tiny black holes
Through which debris may also channel
Like the particles of energy left from snuffed out light
Yet divorced from light
Manifested by sound
A shooting star resolves in a lightless black hole
Ringing through the universe
As sonic vibrations
In a universal sea of humming energy

For the Sake of the Baby in a Manger

I have a responsibility to the public, you know
We all have a responsibility said Chelsea Manning
Who grew up as Bradley Manning
Until she was accepted as a woman
A military judge deemed her innocent seven years ago
Of charges that she aided the enemy
Yet her acts of courage still are taught
In military schools as acts of terrorism
Terrorism to want the public to know how their country deviates
From their own norms of justice and claims of pursuit for peace
Terrorism to inform the public of military attacks on journalists
Of military attacks on civilians of brutality and cover ups
Chelsea Manning still held in prison
As are Assange and Snowden
Although long deemed innocent of charges
Remains an example of injustice at this time of Christmas
When innocence is celebrated
Recognizing we all have a responsibility
To the public, you know
It is time to pardon those who need no pardon
But must be freed for justice
For their sake, for the people
And for the sake of the baby in the manger
Now, at Christmas, or anytime

I Am Oromo

I am Oromo

I live in the Horn of Africa

I live in beautiful Oromia

But I fled invasions into my country

I speak my beautiful Cushitic language

I am native African

My culture and language tell stories

I am Oromo

My country is vast and covers much of Ethiopia

I developed agriculture in this breadbasket of Africa

Fifty years ago people starved in my country

Because of insects and drought

But mostly because of the Ethiopian soldiers

Who confiscated Oromo ancestral land

Left fallow and uncultivated

We were left to starve with most of Ethiopia

If we had not had our land taken away

We would not have starved

We are brilliant farmers and know our land

We know our culture and love our Oromo books

But Ethiopia does not want our children to learn

They do not let us have our books

They do not let our children learn their beautiful language

They do not want our children to learn our culture

I think the powers in Ethiopia do not like us

Maybe they think we are too smart

They turn mercenaries against us

Abyssinians mercenaries and Eritrean mercenaries

Although we have peace treaties with everyone

Once we were the leaders in Oromia

We were respected

We wanted everyone to live in peace

To have books

To be able to farm and learn and live happily

I am Oromo

I am proud of my country

Now young Oromo men hide in the mountains and forests

They are not afraid to die saving our country

But I do not want them to die

I want peace

Democracy is Dying

There was a time the US stood up for human rights
Stood up for democracy
Was willing to say "give me liberty or give me death"
Yet today we abnegate freedom to the Palestinians
Over seventy years under the thumb of Israel
Occupied, incarcerated, treated officially as second class citizens
Now small measures such as boycotts of goods made on
Palestinian land by Israel
Similar to boycotts of South African goods made in the
Bantustans supporting apartheid
Boycotts of goods and any recognition of the legitimacy of South
Africa
Which were welcomed by the west to support a democratic state
Are now condemned by the west as anti-Semitic, racist and
illegal
Israel assassinates the top scientist in Iran
And we look the other way
Israel continues to build settlements on Palestinian land
And we support the illegal settlements
Israel continues to raid homes at night to incarcerate minors in
its prisons
Continues to restrict Palestinian access to water, food and
education

Continues to marginalize Palestinians through check points and absorption of Palestinian farms
Continues to build a wall separating Palestinians from their homes and farms
Continues to shoot Palestinians who congregate at the border to demand their rights
The USA supports Israel in all its deliberate illegal actions
Even the United Nations has revised its list of companies doing business for Israel on Palestinian land
To accommodate the undemocratic wishes of the west
Vice President elect Kamala Harris says Israel must be supported in its occupation of Palestine
In its wall, its bulldozing of Palestinian villages to create its own settlements, its apartheid, its prisons
Secretary of State Pompeo would rewrite the book on Israeli illegal activities
President Trump would rewrite the Constitution demanding that everyone be counted in a census
The same president who seems to feel democratic elections should be ignored to make him president again
Because the USA no longer supports democracy
Democracy is dying in the USA
Bring flowers to pour them on the tombstones of democracy in America

You are more than you

You are more than you
Poet philosopher gardener vintner
Engineer chef fisherman
Hermit I want to know
Fellow spirit on life's walk
A shell closed
To a myriad of pearls
Of consciousness
You are more than you
Idea thought artist
Carver of dams and breakwaters
That demand to be respected
Planner of patterns of ideas
Like those on the flute of Pan
Played for the beauty of earth
You are more than you
Magician dreamer lover
Unopened book I touch
Unopened package
Tied with strings of pain and joy
Containing my heart
You are more than you
A house a window
Diamond Head in Hawaii

A valley in Lake County

You are the Rockies

Oceans and tsunamis

Rivers, shores, and coastlines

You are China and France

A journey a destination

A crumpled piece of paper

A smile an enigmatic look

And I look for all the pieces

That are more than you

All the pieces

To mold them around

The only you

I know

Reaching into Fog

I see fog out the window
I hear the groan of the fog horn
Birds cower still under the eaves
I am alone with my memories
I am alone with the fog
I wrap myself in the idea of clouds
And wait for blue
Blue peeks through mist
As I reach out
Like ripe fruit
Squeezing itself into the dawn
Dripping into a waiting world
Holding all that I am
Sour and sweet
Mixing through clouds
Into the marrow of dreams
Skeletal fragments
Begging to be joined
In the blind space of fog
Begging to be whole
In the haunting dream
Of fog
Begging to be found within
Narrow piping over hearts of fire

Burning in an unseen well

Of silence

Seeking truth beyond the fog

Seeking eyes to see

Into the marrow of a heart

Held by fragments

Suffused with drops of my own soul

Consumed by fog

Congress on the Bay

A ferry floats

Chugs pushes

Through dappled waters

Towards a pier

A man with a Boston accent

Expounds upon the dock

Expounds on Aristotle

Dark matter time travel

Transformation heresy

Live streaming verbiage

Floats past the ferry

Past the birds

Flies over the blue and white ferry

Now backing out

Revving its engines

To face again the bay

Passing another ferry

Passing gulls

Squabbling squeaking singing

Joining the cacophony

Of philosophic verbiage

With their own raucous

Commentary

A pelican enters the picture

Over a small sailboat

The afternoon wanes

As small birds

Dare to appear

Where gulls

Had just held

Congress

Alcatraz

Hundreds of gulls
Escape Alcatraz
Stream over the blinking
Prison tower
Standing guard over
Hills ridges cliffs
History
An island
Once home to Ohlone
Then home to prisoners
Home to Wei Wei
Home to art
To colonial seabirds
Cormorants
Alcatraces
Meaning
Strange bird
Or Pelican
Or even
Lilies
Flowers
And birds
Are free
On Alcatraz

Dreams and Glass

She speaks slowly

Dreaming perhaps

Her feet are bandaged

She leans forward

In her wheelchair

Fish in the aquarium

Seem empathic arbiters

Of possible navigation

Journeys in water

Journeys in dreams

Viewed outward

From an inner world

Surreal ambience

Weightless movement

Through water as through space

Through dreams

Memories untouchable

Dreamable

Evening housekeeping

Brooms brush by

Glass windows

Glass fish tanks

Glass walls

Separate

Dreams

From reality

Brooms

From swimming fish

Urban movement

From a still suspension

Outside noises

Passersby

Live today without dreams

Separated by glass

From dreamers

Dreaming

Glass boxes

Contain worlds

Separating

The dreamer

From the dream

Yesterday

From today

Tomorrow

From tomorrow

A Damp Dawn

The sky is damp with morning clouds
Birds question the morning with tiny chirps
A sun has risen behind an opaque veil
Not yet ready to enter a dark city
Blossoms gently peek out from tight cups
Unsure of their welcome in gray dawn
Yet soft tendrils of light venture out
Like moments quick with wisdom dare to share
Some insight like delayed flights of birds
Attempt to ride the wind and meet the sun
Pushing against dawn's reluctance to be day
As we too push against our fears
Accept a dawn of sullen clouds and tears
And join the birds in morning flight
Encouraging the sun to give us light

Lashes in Saudi Arabia

In Saudi Arabia
A bird's cries
Are silenced
In prison
For ten years
A bird's wings
Offer no refuge
For 1000 lashes
From a flogging cane
Raif Badawi
Condemned for blogging words
Words considered insulting
To a prophet
Caged and lashed
Flesh made sore
Word from flesh
The whip of a cane cannot end
The journey of a pen
Nor prison
Gag its message

(From Amnesty International Website)

"…..Despite a powerful global outcry, Raif Badawi was flogged this morning after morning prayers in Jeddah. An eyewitness shared his account of Raif's brutal flogging with Amnesty. It's almost too difficult to read.
"Raif was escorted from a bus and placed in the middle of the crowd, guarded by eight or nine officers. He was handcuffed and shackled but his face was not covered - everyone could see his face...
A security officer approached him from behind with a huge cane and started beating him.
Raif raised his head towards the sky, closing his eyes and arching his back. He was silent, but you could tell from his face and his body that he was in real pain.
The officer beat Raif on his back and legs, counting the lashes until they reached 50.
The punishment took about 5 minutes. It was very quick, with no break in between lashes."Saudi Arabian authorities' decision to inflict such a vicious, cruel form of punishment on a nonviolent activist like Raif is shocking. But it is imperative that we neither look away from such cruelty, nor be shocked into silence.
Raif's ordeal is only beginning - he is scheduled to be flogged another 950 times over the next 19 weeks. This means that our work as activists is also just beginning. In response to the Saudi authorities' brutality….."

Anti-Bias Training by the Wiesenthal Center

California State Superintendent of Schools
Tony Thurmond
Wants to give our children anti-bias training
By the Simon Wiesenthal Center
Founded to advocate for Israel
A country specifically created to privilege one group over others
A country whose state ideology is termed racist by most of the world
A country who continuously suppresses those people it considers inferior to the Jews
Those allocated privilege and citizenship over a people whose country they annexed
Who takes the money of Palestinians to be held in trust for their needs yet will not give it back
Who confiscates tools they purchase to rebuild their infrastructure
To build schools and desalination plants
Who kills them when they approach their own farms or play on their own beaches
Who raids their homes for young children to put in prisons that torture and maim
A country whose founding in 1948 was based on "ethnic cleansing"
Cleansing Palestine of its indigenous population to create Israel

An act counter to our international treaties, counter to our own domestic polices and the Charter of the United Nations
A country who oppresses and denies basic human rights to those whose country they stole
A country that receives over $10 million per day of American taxes
Thanks to the super lobby for Israel and AIPAC
A country whom we want our school children to respect
A country whose ideology we want our school children to emulate and absorb
A country whose goal is to rid itself of its indigenous population
Through any means possible
A Center devoted to advocacy for such a country
Should teach our children not to discriminate?
Putting the Wiesenthal Center in charge of teaching our children compassion
Is like putting the coyote in charge of the ducklings
Or the fox in charge of the hens

Gillnets and Mercury

California's swordfish
Are caught in
Large-scale drift gillnets
Known to catch
Dolphins, porpoises
Leatherback turtles
Sperm whales
All endangered species
Intelligent species
Whom we love
To whom we continue
To feed mercury
Through our industrial waste
Yet swordfish
Whom our fisheries covet
And King Mackerel and Tilefish
Contain more mercury than any other fish
And yet fisheries still catch them
Along with the dolphins and sperm whales
Who get locked in the gillnets
And put them on our tables
For consumption
Doing little
To rid the oceans

Of mercury

And gillnets

Although California

Is the last

Of our fishing industries

To use the

Murderous

Gillnets

It is not the last

To catch fish

Soaked in mercury

To place at our tables

Turtle trapped in gillnet

Summer Scene

Across the street

The green, glistening tree

Dappled with shadows and yellow glints of sparkling light

Sports red, black, brown and blue patches among its leaves,

Dancing in the light summer wind

A softly murmuring Burberry neighbor

Bends over quietly

As if sheltering its green cousin,

Speaking sweet nothings

The bells of summer

Knell beyond this simple scene

With ringing notes

Awakening hibernating life

The cat lies

Soft salt and peppered back paws splayed

Tail limp

Front paws, pure white mittens,

Beating the air gently

One after the other

As if climbing a staircase

In the air

Or perhaps swimming

Treading air as if it were water

Eyes closed partially

Just a sliver open

Dreaming

Meditating

Or contemplating

A mouse or mole

Every morning

4 am

The bird above my window

Sings

Until this morning

I look up after dawn

Into her most precarious nest

And pray that all is well

Perhaps she merely follows

Her young offspring

Into an unknown

And most precarious

World

Ozon

The Greek word to smell
Created our word Ozone
To commemorate the
Fresh
Clean
Smell
After a storm
Like an enriched smell
Of oxygen
Permeating the world
As we imagine
A whole layer of ozone
In danger of becoming
A porous rag
Due to our own refrigeration systems
And thoughtless actions
Here on earth
Stretching over our world
Smelling like
Rain
Asking only to bless us all
And remain Ozone
And retain the wings
Of angels

Within a Flower

Within a flower
Velvet intricacies
Folded petals
Open to delicate stamen
Welcoming bees
And hummingbirds
Into a dance pf destiny
Shedding pollens
Breathing perfumes
Inspiring bouquets
Wreaths
Garlands
Leis
And sneezes
Within a flower
Fairies dream
And spin with spiders
Airy schemes
Of floral scents
Etched to entice
A bee or two
Or merely to
Accompany a symphony
Led by the wind

Warmed by the sun
On violins
And harps plucked by
Angelic fingers
Lingering at
Glissando heights
While fairy wings
Brush by the sight
Of flowers
Tucking
Into night

Somalia

Balanced on a rope of love
Cushitic Waaq
A cow who turned away
Bringing disaster
The rope of love
Between two horns
Eternal Waaq
Must be restored
Arawelo
Queen who like the Greeks
Bade her women
Bind themselves
Refuse themselves
To men
Until war
Might cease
She who was
The female horn
Of God
And still
A mortal queen
Would restore balance
Dancing on a rope

Of love

For peace

The first Homo sapiens

Came from Somalia

Where agriculture

Was sustainable

People thrived

Wrote poetry

And danced

Until the imperialist dragons

Broke their instruments

Imposed servitude

Indebtedness

Trampled on their beauty

Took their land and harvests

So they might starve

Genocide by International Monetary Fund

Which took all they had

All they had given the world

Science art language government

Gender equality

Returning these gifts

With disease and starvation

Somalia

Fecund

Rich in beauty

In land poetry and people
Cowers under the fiery breath
Of the imperialist dragon
Cowers under the whip
Of its greedy rider
Corporate robot
Riding the dragon of imperialism
To a world of dust
Somalia
Balanced on a rope of love
Swing wide
Return to grace
Return to the garden
Of Arawelo
Force the dragon
Back into its cave
Look again with love
Upon the bull that waits
Waits for eternal Waaq
Eternal harmony
Somalia

The Sight of the Child

Follow the light
Follow the sight of the child
Who sees what is right
Whose image of life is simply what is
The light that shows colors
Shows brightness shows people
Bathed only in light
As they march through their lives
Look in the eyes of a child
Look where its eyes look
In trust and in faith
Pray for that child
Pray no harm befall it
That it never may learn
Not to trust in this world
That it carry the message
Of love and of truth
Seeing even in evil
A corner of light
To hide in reside in
So all may be well
So all may be true
So all may be light
In the sight of the child

Waiting for the Storm

The storm is hiding

Under or perhaps behind

The sunset

The glorious sunset

Waving goodbye

to bright

Luminescent sunshine

Drawing shadows

Closed

The night is silent

Waiting

For the

Storm

Rain Continues

Rain continues
Obliquely insistent
Yet hesitantly apologetic
Knowing her slanted siege
Was unexpected
To all who welcomed
Clear blue morning skies

100 000 Poets for Change

100 000 poets for change
With poetry ask for homes for refugees
With poetry ask for justice
With poetry ask for an end to police murder
With poetry scream that the vulnerable matter
Black lives matter
George Floyd matters
Children matter
Health care matters
Education and school books
Tell the world that a pandemic changes everything
That prisons and elderly homes should be emptied
Workers sent home from processing plants
People not forced to die
100 000 Poets for Change
Offers a Madonna and child for our era
Like the Madonna and child
Two thousand years ago
Reflecting compassion and love
In the face of pain and suffering
A child taken from her mother
At the border
Perhaps never to see her again
Or left to sicken and die

A Madonna and child
Aware of the suffering of the world
100 000 poets for change
Demand children be reunited
Demand children not be separated
From their families
100 000 poets for change
Demand an end to war
An end to bombs killing children
And their grannies
Reaching out to embrace them
Turned to dust in a flash
An end to bombs
Murdering people celebrating a wedding
Killing ill and disabled in hospitals
Children going to school
100 000 poets for change
Demand an end to torture
An end to prisons that punish
To prisons that do not heal
An end to injustice
To occupation to murder
Demand a new world
A world of kindness
A world of gardens
Free of pesticides

A world of oceans

Free of pollution and acid

An earth free of drilling into its heart

Events all over the world

Every fourth week in September

Cry out for change

Cry out with poetry

Cry out with words

For justice and healing

Their only weapons

A pen

Ink

And love

The Year Rolls Out

The year rolls out
Gently
In the cold night
Reluctantly
Acquiescing
To the inevitable
Sliding between worlds
Imagining a crack to repair
Like a hair fracture
A prayer
A wish to be renewed
In grace
Seeking absolution
Tracing her path in the stars
So far away
Yet giving light
Radiating warmth into a universe
Indifferent to time
To rolling of the years
Yet carried tenderly
By angels
The cat is awake
Tracing her own path
Through chill morning air

Aware of dawn's whispers

Mist disappearing

With dew dampening her fur

Evaporating

Dreams

Scenes of a Rainy Night

Rain accompanies us

Accompanies the car

Dancing with the wind shield wipers

Up and down

Beating at the windows

And the canvas

Stretched over the convertible

Beating

Beating

Pleading

To come in

Just a drop

Or two?

The storm was spent

After howling

Frantically spinning

Beating against its own

Impatience

Whipping

Its own wetness

To exhaustion

Dripping now

From tree to tree

Softly

Plopping

On the leaves

And rivulets

Streaming

Through

Gutters

Of a softened city

The dawn came softly

Clouds of

Rose and peach

Cotton streams

Of rosy color

Commanding all

The sky

As if that

Were

Its stage

At dawn

My hands rest

On the computer's keyboard

A ring on the left hand

Gnarled with raised veins

Soft knuckles

Close cut nails

To play the piano

On a different

Keyboard

After

Gazing out

Upon a drenched

Yet rosy

Day

Conjunction of Jupiter and Saturn

About every three hundred years
Jupiter and Saturn converge for our eyes
Close enough to create a spectacular event
In the night sky
This year 2020 we see the conjunction
As happened three times in the year 7 BC
Made visible in the East
To give reason for the Magi to start for Bethlehem
A second conjunction in September might have urged them on
A third and final meeting of Saturn and Jupiter in December
Happened as they met with King Herod in Judea
Who sent them on to seek diligently for the young child
"That he might worship him"
But instead sent his soldiers on a mission
Remembered as the slaughter of the innocents in art and story
Three celestial meetings of the two bright planets
In one year that might have seen the birth of Jesus
Led scholars and monks to wonder at the synchronicity of events
And today for us to look for signs of hope in the heavens
As we look for light beyond the present miasma of plague
Light to guide us into the new year
Watching the skies in wonder at the conjunction of two planets
And in prayer that the joining of Jupiter and Saturn
The supreme god of thunder and lightning and storms

And the god of seed and replenishment

God of springtime and the sewing of incipient growth

With the god of might

Two gods who often morphed in legend

And every three centuries in our skies

Might glow over us now

And usher in a year of blessing

Christmas Tree in Beirut

There is an enormous Christmas tree

At the port in Beirut

At the scene where a small fire lit

A vast explosion

Killing 150 people

Including all emergency firefighters

Injuring thousands more

An enormous tree stands in Lebanon

At the port

Decorated with the jackets

And hard hats

Of firefighters

Who died August 4, 2020

In the midst of a pandemic

At the port

Where deadly nitrates had been stored

For seven years

Stored and waiting like a giant tinder box

Waiting for a small fire

To blast open a waiting warehouse

And kill 150 people

And firefighters

Who were given no instructions

As to where the fire was

Given no instructions

As to the deadly explosives

Waiting seven years in the warehouse

Given no keys to the warehouse

Where the small fire was smoldering

Given insufficient water

Forced to improvise

And die

To be commemorated this Christmas

With an enormous tree

Hung with their jackets

And red hard hats

For firefighters

And all others who died

Killed in an explosion

In Beirut

I Walk Through the Garden

I walk through the garden
Absorbing flowers
Tasting yellows
Hearing blues
Subsuming green
Through my boots
The daisies sway east and west
Blown into daisy tai chi
Forward and back
Leaves raised
Undulating and bowing
As I return their bow
And dance with them
Under clouds shot with sunshine
I walk through the garden
Leaves crunching under my boots
Yellow-rumped warblers
Dart from branch to branch
Perched pecking
Climbing gamboling
Like stemless flowers
In constant motion
A ruby crowned kinglet
Sees me with her big eyes

Jumps back
Showing her ruby cap
Like a touch of red velvet
Or pomegranate
While the mocking bird
Rises on her glorious wings
Black and white
Against a symphony
Of color
I walk through the garden
Absorbing sweetness

Northern Spool

Viewing our blue planet from space

We see Greenland

Part of Denmark

The top of Europe

Greenland warming rapidly

The Arctic warming rapidly

Bering Sea elders adapt

They hunt on thin ice

Ships now traffic the Arctic

Seeing no ice

Like a spool spinning out

Ice melts more quickly

Spinning out the spools

Of our poles

Turning our poles

Into lakes

Of empty spools

While we see only blue

From outer space

Global Events

Kilauea spews again
Red lava flows
In time for the winter solstice
In time for the conjunction
Of Jupiter and Saturn
Pandemic morphs in England
Forcing more shutdowns
People flock to Mexico
Not shut down
Not requiring quarantines
Beautiful beaches
Open to the world
Christmas week 2020
The Arctic melts
Plastic remains in the ocean
Refugees drown
Or march for their rights
As the pandemic
Still rages
Throughout
A warming
World

A Christmas Star

The crescent moon hung
Inquisitively
Her profile gently curved
Looking down just slightly
Toward Jupiter and Saturn
Two planets whose orbits
Had remained apart
Eight hundred years
Dancing towards each other
In the evening sky
Jupiter brightly glowing
Saturn more shyly twirling her rings
An orange and purple sunset
Spread beneath them
As they brightened the night
Two planets converging
Sometimes called the Christmas Star
For their meeting three times
In the year Jesus may have been born
Said to have led the wise men
On their journey east
Towards a manger
Towards shepherds and angels
Towards a story

Made more brilliant

By the shining

Of two planets

Converging with the glow

As of a radiant star

Journalists Killed

In 2020

The year of protests and pandemic

Journalists are targeted

For telling truth to power

Over two hundred languish

In prisons around the world

Iran, Afghanistan, Syria, Philippines

And especially Mexico

Targets journalists

Targets truth

Where truth is suppressed

Or scoffed

The atmosphere is ripe

For the repression of journalists

Where presidents

And global leaders

Tell lies

The atmosphere is ripe

Globally

For the repression of truth

Police target protesters

Pepper spray journalists

Trump calls

"Lamestream media"

Truth walks the streets

On the curbs

And in doorways

Simply trying

To survive

Malalalai Maiwand,

Afghan TV and radio reporter

Fatally shot on her way to work

Among the thirty shot in Afghanistan

Ruhollah Zam, journalist in Iran

Killed this month

For reporting on protests two years ago

Thirty journalists

Assassinated in the Philippines

Nineteen gunned down in Mexico

This year alone

Thirty-four killed in Russia

Since Puten came to power

Numerous journalists killed

In the United States

Including twenty-six last year

Two killed

During an online interview

Six in a TV tower during a broadcast

Four killed in a news office in Maryland

Hundreds harassed

Beaten by police

Cameras confiscated

Truth gets up each morning

Stretches into the sunshine

Walks the streets

Always fearing

The next bullet

Journalists demonstrate against murder of colleague in Mexico

Legend of Mount Kelimutu. Indonesia

There is a volcano in Indonesia

Mount Kelimutu

Rising over three crater lakes of three colors

Turquoise, red and dark blue

Spirits dwell in these lakes

Revered by the natives

As legend tells

There were two witches

An evil witch Ata Polo

And a good witch Ata Mbutu

Two orphan children were pursued by Ata Polo

Thinking to have them as a treat

But they ran to Ata Mbutu

Who protected them against the evil witch

Promising to give them up when they were grown

They grew strong and beautiful

And hid in a cave in Mount Kelimutu

Who sheltered them as his mountain children

Ata Polo was so angry

He turned Mbutu into green stones

And threw them into one crater

Making the water green

Becoming the lake of the elders and wisdom

Tiwu Ata Mbutu

But his anger was so hot
Ata Polo burned and rolled down the mountain
Turning the water of another crater red
Making it the destination for evil spirits
Tiwu Ata Polo
While the children came out of their caves
To swim in the third crater
Beautiful and filled with turquoise water
It became known as
The lake of young men and maidens
Tiwu Nua Muri Kooh Tai
Sometimes the lake bubbles
When the spirits of children play in its waters
And so three lakes of different colors
Tell the legend of the great volcano
Mount Kelimutu
And its sacred craters

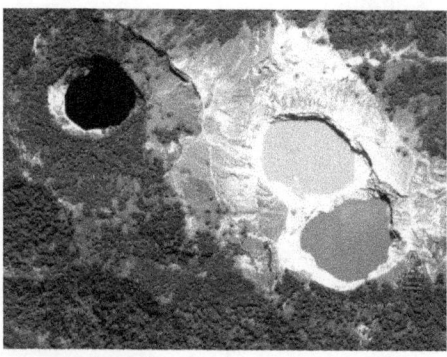

Mongolia

Embracing the great Khangai mountains
Cradling lakes of the clearest water in the world
One called Blue Pearl
Fished in summer or through deep ice in winter
Strung with rivers
Along its Siberian border with Russia
Where six foot long salmon swim
Called Taimon
Large enough to devour beavers
Fished thousands of years by nomads
Hunters and warriors of its taiga
Home to herds of reindeer
Enlisted by our Santa Claus
For a winter sleigh ride with legendary toys
Visited by musk deer with fierce canine teeth
Instead of antlers
Who live in its vast cedar forests
Northern Mongolia
Remains a mystery
A great taiga
Reaching south to the Gobi desert
A giant palm
Holding pristine mountains, forest and lakes
Cupped to contain beauty and magic

History of conquerors and survivors

Intersecting stories of Russia and China

Meeting in the lines

Drawn by nomads

And the army of Genghis Khan

Fertile land for conquest

A crossroads between Asia and Europe

Full of story and legend

Coins

Follow the money they say

Follow the money

Empty as it may be of value

Trade proceeds to representatives of trade

Coinage or valuable minerals

Precious for being rare and beautiful

Or useful as tools

Traded for knots on wampum

Traded for cloth

Traded for paper

Traded for numbers in a bank

Or numbers in a cloud

Evolving into algorithms

Traded as bitcoins

Valuable because they are believed

To be valuable

Wealth continuously evolving

In an i-cloud of mystery

Now pennies or nickels or dimes

Early coinage can be traded for large sums

As tactile representatives

Of what was once

A trade of a goat

For a barrel of apples

Christmas Scene

Christmas clouds float in a blue sky
Dried out from yesterday's rain
Promenading slowly past tall buildings
A raven quarrels with a telephone pole
Lifting itself off with fanning wings
Reaching towards blue
Small birds hold court on cables
Babbling sweet nothings
A stuffed bear views the scene
Gazing across at holiday lights
Bleached out red cap with white tassel
Hanging over his white shoulders
He remembers a glorious red sunrise
And wonders how the sun managed
Such a magnificent performance
With so little preparation
And cleaned off the stage so quickly
Pulling back the curtain to a blue scene
With clouds floating in the eaves

Finding Vision

A new year
Draws the curtain on 2020
A term used to represent perfect vision
Something our world needs
Vision to see imperfection
Vision to see the poor
Vision to see the vulnerable
Vision to see who must be helped
To see who needs homes
To see who needs safety
To see who must be protected
To see what we must still learn
Vision to see what needs healing
Vision to see what is real
Presbyopia vision clouds our thought
Requiring correction of the heart
Until we can see what is close
Until we can see and touch and feel
Until we can observe with the eyes
Of all humanity
We cannot begin the work
To heal our world
We cannot begin the work
To feed the hungry

To release the prisoner

To unite children and families

To embrace justice

Until we can see with our hearts

We cannot begin the work

To heal our soul

And the soul of the world

Going to Mars

We want to go to Mars
Fertile ground for science fiction
Visions of water and old civilizations
God of war for Greek story tellers
Lover of Venus
Whom he meets in the skies
Sometimes aligned with Mercury
Jupiter and Saturn
All gods for poets who tell stories
Of the heavens
We want to visit Mars
Everyone wants to land on Mars
To answer questions
About a planet so close
And accessible
We want to camp on Mars
With nuclear energy
To power our campsite
Yet we argue that someone
Maybe a Martian
Will steal its fuel
To build a bomb
So perhaps we are not ready
Perhaps we are not yet adults

Ready to build together
Ready to work together
In peace
Perhaps we are still too foolish
To play together
As adults
To build a campsite
And a very special campfire
We know how to build
Together
With molten salt or
With sodium and
Maybe highly enriched uranium
To burn safely for years
To energize a campsite
We all want to build
Someday
On Mars

Pomegranate

Plump round pushing crisp skin
Pomegranates are said to have 618 arils
The number of commandments in Torah
Genesis tells of pomegranates
Brewed with wheat and barley
After squeezing their juices by hand
To create a sacred beverage
A pomegranate calyx crowns the high priest
Whose robe is embroidered with designs
Of barley, wheat and pomegranates
Bounty of the land of milk and honey
Mohammed claims eating pomegranate seeds
Cleanses us from hatred and envy
Greeks recommend pomegranate for fertility
Buddha for curing evil
Persian hero Isfandiyar consumes a pomegranate
Becoming invincible
Becoming Isfahan, golden city of Iran
While golden pomegranates adorn spears and temples
Fruit of healing
Fruit of sanctity
Pomegranate remains the
Ruby jewel of taste and beauty
Ruby jewel of life

Light on the Ganges

Candles burning from dried leaf bowls
Float along the holy Ganges
Reflecting inner light and outer beauty
While Ghats lining the Ganges
Shine with candles
Flickering through smoke ascending
As spirits from their ashen shells
I set my candle in its bowl upon the holy river
Watching it follow other candles
In a stream of holiness
Fingers of smoke
Rise above the candles
As the Ganges becomes
A Divali of prayer
For all who bathe in its light

Pain

I bruised my rib yesterday
A slight bruise
Achieved by reaching for supplies
On the bottom shelf at a grocery store
I had to sleep on my back
Not to feel the bruise
And thought how small pains
Remind us of our humanity
Remind us of how we always
Might do something differently
But we will all endure pain
We will all endure heartbreak
We will all have the opportunity
To endure the pains of others
And that is perhaps the reason for pain
The crack in our perfect world
That allows pain
That allows children to endure loss
And suffering no way deserved
That allows them to drown
In the Mediterranean
And be washed up on European shores
That we may share the pain
The crack in our perfect world

That we create ourselves

Through our governments

Through our greed

The crack in our perfect world

That allows pain

The crack that we create

In our own hearts

And fail to repair

The crack that allows pain

And opens our understanding

So that we might feed love

So that we might feed joy

Into that crack

To heal the pain

To repair the world

My Journey

Today I start a journey into my heart
I look for a door or a window
But find only a crack
I need to climb through
To find my way into a cave of confusion
To walk through tunnels
Lit only with my imagination
I start a journey into my heart
Offering myriads of pathways
To unknown destinations
Lit only with candles of ideas
I stumble on my journey
Over roots left by my past
Regrets and anguish
Languishing still in soils of my heart
Shooting upwards
Seeking renewal
Seeking to turn injury into healing
I start a journey into my heart
Which will always be a beginning
I kiss the roots over which I have stumbled
And embrace the wisdom they have found
Growing through anger and confusion
Into long arms of love

Reaching within my heart
Where I walk blindly
Seeing only the shadows left by flickering candles
Leaning against tunnel walls
Following shadows
Leading me upwards through my heart
Pumping me eternally
Pushing me infinitely
Into veins of joy

Halos on a City

The sun is shining
So brightly I cannot see the buildings across the street
They are simply illumination
Reflected by the sun
Halos on a city
Deeply in need of spiritual renewal
Deeply in need of illumination
Deeply in need of angels
Who might knit its heart together
Who might thread its vulnerable
Into homes and safety
Angels who might teach us
To feed its hungry children
To sustain its mothers and families
Who might teach us
To allow the poor to live without fear
Teach us to banish poverty
And excess wealth
That all might thrive
Under blinding sunshine
In a city deeply in need of angels
Deeply in need of illumination
Illumination that does not blind the spirit
To love

The Cold Wolf Moon

Tonight the full moon rides

To the top of the sky

A glowing round face

Beams its bright cheeks

Almost at death-defying heights

A trapeze artist at the top of her swing

A shining golden globe

Caught just beyond the Pleiades

Who decide to accompany her

On her journey over a shadow world

Seven sisters paying court to their queen

A splendid moon

Bidding goodbye to the year

From the top of the sky

While embroidered clouds

Slide like silver jewels across her velvet gown

And somewhere in the cold north

Wolves howl at the full ice moon

As she beams from the pinnacle of moon heaven

Sent with a slingshot

So high the seven sisters

Laugh at her daring

On her year's final ride

Through a dark winter night

Blessing

Last night I saw a bluebird
A western bluebird I had been watching for
Then there were two and three
With blushing faint red bibs
Chirping making flying loops
From chapel roof to cabbage palm tree
I felt blessed as I walked into the garden
Filled the birdbath
And suddenly a tiny bushtit appeared
From nowhere
To peck and try the water
While seven bushtit friends
All congregated in the birdbath
Gently twittering
As I walked out I saw the sun begin to set
Golden globe slipping behind the horizon
And sat watching it from the car
While a boys choir sang on the radio
In Paradisum
From Faure's Requiem
A blessing for a world
At home in its own glory

Gratitude and Awe

Yesterday I thought about gratitude
And realized I am not just grateful
For nature and love and beauty
It is far more than that
I am deeply in awe of light
And the flutter of wings of birds
The song of the sparrow
The thrusting of a blade of grass
Piercing the earth fully formed
With spear and shield
Tiny yet perfect
I am deeply in awe of a child's smile
Of the rise and fall of constellations
As the universe polishes its own gears
Adjusting its infinitude of movement
I am deeply in awe of the pen of
Bach and Beethoven
The music of Bernstein and Bartok
The growth of music from a reed in the forest
The rattle of gourds
The wailing and pounding of the earth
With feet and hands
To jazz and symphony
Calliope and combo

The pen of Shakespeare
And the poem of a child
Relating to what is more than magic
Asking where we come from
And where we are going
And I do not know
But I am more than grateful
That I am present
And can hear the question
And remain in awe

Visiting Golden Gate Park

Visiting Golden Gate Park
During a pandemic
Means getting lost between
Streets that are open and
Those that are closed
Getting lost to find surprises
Of bushes blooming in December
Of giant maple trees
And Monterey Pines
And lakes hiding in plain sight
Next to the road
Mallard Lake growing a giant tree
Out of its marshy beauty
Bending like a father over
Mallards male and female
And coots pumping themselves
Across a living lake
Elk Lake across the street
Offering clear waters to December resident
And migratory birds
Spreading its arms as the native she is
To embrace her flying
Climbing swimming children
Living in her womb

No Space for Grief

Grief has no space

In pandemic times

For stages of denial

Or anger

No space for bargaining

No chance to trade a virus

For something else

No space for depression

As friends or relatives succumb

To illness

Or simply remain unseen

In quarantine

Or hiding behind masks

Distanced and outside

Protecting themselves

And others

From an uninvited

Visitor

Who cannot be banned

Until science

Itself can

Wring out grief

Wipe away its tears

For whose stages

We have

No space

For whose source

We can only seek

Extermination

By science

By vaccinations

Or mutation

Into a safe variant

Demanding no stages

Of grief

For which we have

No time

For which we have

No space

Less or More

The New Year is upon us
A pandemic still raging
People walking about in masks
Careful or not careful
To distance themselves from others
One reads that the safe distance
From a gorilla so as not to contaminate
Is 23 feet, or 35 feet without a mask
For humans it is 6 feet with or without mask
Humans are not an endangered species
The New Year is upon us
We read of minimalism
Less is more
Get rid of everything you don't need
How do you know what you don't need?
I see papers from twenty years ago
That bring back memories
As I declutter my home
I see manuscripts and letters
Lost in re-filing
Lost in the squeezing together of space
After loss of the reason for space
The reason for each day having meaning
I declutter and repurpose

I look about my minimal alone
Minimal touch
Minimal speech
Minimal me
And wonder if less is more
If less is a shrinking of being
If less and less
Eventually shrinks
Into nothingness
Or moves into another space
Of knowledge
Of reassessment of loss
Into a gain of insight
Into a gain of awareness
Of our vulnerability
Of our love of each other
Of our need to care
For each other
And for ourselves
And for something
Greater than less
Greater than more

A Tiny Story

The sun shines brightly
On a New Year
Clouds sit lethargically
Rags on a morning sky
Resting in place
Nowhere to go
Wondering if a wind
Will move them somewhere
East or west
A lonely bird sits upon a cable
Still and quiet
Until I hear a tiny chirp
And see his small head move side to side
Looking for company
A friend answers his chirp
From a telephone pole
I wonder if birds have nests
In telephone poles
Three birds fly in to perch on the pole
The lonely bird joins them
As the rags in the sky are subsumed by pale blue
And fade into a watercolor wash
Canvas waiting to be painted
For the New Year

Marguerite

Loves me loves me not
Petals on a daisy
Asking the eternal question
The plucking fingers
As puzzled as the daisy
Yet wanting the last petal
To say yes
To say loves me
As we all yearn
For something we do not understand
Yet consumes us
The desire to be desired
As the petals fall to earth
Ignorant of their message
Themselves discarded
Though perhaps conveyers
Of a ticket to happiness or grief
Regardless of how the last petal
Falls

A Door

He is gone or passed or perhaps dead
Although I do not speak the word
Because it seems so absolute
I know a door has closed
Which might contain his spirit
Although his spirit is far beyond
Closed doors
The door of his warmth is closed
The door of his smile is closed
The door of his touch is closed
The handle on the door does not move
The door is cold to the touch
And asks me to turn around
Asks me to turn my face to the sky
Asks me to let the sun shine on my face
Asks me to find warmth in the sun and
The touch of all that is alive
Asks me to let go of the handle of the door
Asks me to live with the living
Asks me to let his love open me to life
That he might live again
Through me

Love

She wondered if she might love another
But she was too hesitant
And another found a lover
She thought she might love another
But she was unsure of her grief
And whether he who had passed
Would ever forgive
Her embracing one other
Than her forever lover
Who was no longer corporeal
Yet love is strangely tolerant
Neither jealous nor proud
Love does not ask questions
Nor demand conditions
Love embraces all
Forgives as if there were never a need
For forgiveness
Love extends into love
A nebula of love
Exploding and embracing
A universe of longing for love
A universe defined by love
And kindness
Ineffable and infinite

New Years 2021

New Years Eve 2021
Strangely bare
Unpopulated
Times Square empty
The ball falls to lights and numbers
Perhaps only virtually
From another year
Photos of people kissing
From another year
A rare bare Times Square
Waiting for a cat
To look for morsels
Left by no one
Surfing on the computer
For scenes of New Years
Fireworks and celebrations
Meeting more virtual displays
On empty streets
A pandemic New Years
A lockdown New Years
A never New Years
And yet 2020 does slide into 2021
Reluctantly pushed from one calendar
Into another

2021 takes the stage

Unsure of her lines

Humble yet hopeful

Her scenes will illuminate

A year of grace

Arm of Fog

The day after New Years
An arm of deep fog
Stretches across chilly hills
Still damp from light rain
A low sky is invisible
Hidden by the arm of fog
Resting on tops of buildings
Curling around wet streets
Trees deserted by birds
Snuggling down in holes
Crevices eaves
Venturing briefly outside
To seek a wayward insect
Or peck a leaf
Plumping feathers
For air waves of warmth
Tucking a foot
Into a downy belly
While eyes peer briefly
Out through
The cool arm of fog
Wrapped around holes
Eaves and crevices
In damp embrace

I often focus in my poetry on how ancient kingdoms and countries are affected by wars, colonization, or other historical and cultural developments. Four of those poems have preceded those you will find scattered to the end of this book.

Kashmir

Like a fur cap
Kashmir sits upon India and Pakistan
While China leans down and curls through
Seeking to connect its own peoples
Through this cap
With its glacial Himalayas
Its great waters
Birthed from an ancient lake
An old kingdom
As old as its Sanskrit name
British held once in its power
Creating modern Kashmir
Through treaty
As traders with their camels
Padded through the mountains and plains
Of this furry cap
Grateful for ambiguous borders
Allowing trade with neighbors
Allowing religions to thrive
Hindu Buddhist Muslim

Yet Pakistan and India
Upon which it sits
Needed its rivers to survive
Needed the rivers of Kashmir
Needed the waters of a great canal
Called Kutte Koi after
Medieval Queen Kuta Rani
Who built the canal
To save her city Shrinagal
From flooding
Necessity birthed anguish
Soldiers pulled and twisted
The beautiful cap of Kashmir
To wring out its waters
To demand its land
Soldiers under the orders
Of India Pakistan China
Cut through the cap of Kashmir
Oblivious to the pain
Of an ancient kingdom
Whose people
Objecting to insufficient treaties
Hug their fur cap
Throw stones at soldiers
And are met with rubber bullets
Leaving permanent damage or death

Tearing away at the fragment

Of a fur cap

Sliding over the forehead

Of Pakistan and India

Or perhaps a Kashmir cap

From a goat

Roaming Ladakh or Baltistan

Settling on the brow of India and Pakistan

Enduring the pain of ages

But wanting only

To be left alone

Sri Lanka

Balangoda bones

Lay buried in Sri Lanka

125,000 years long

Lying under civilizations

Buddhist and Hindu

Sinhalese and Tamil

Kingdoms and dominions

Fighting and creating

Speaking their own language

After their island separates from India

Five to Twenty-five million years ago

Allowing an island culture to grow

Offering many shorelines for foreign vessels

Trading its textiles and spices

For wares of the Portuguese, Greeks, Persians,

Romans, Arabs, Malay, Armenian, Chinese

All who come by water

Prince Vijaya, exiled from India

Sets up a monarchy in Sri Lanka

Buddhism becomes dominant

Yet kingdoms rise and fall

Hydraulic systems in the dry land

Determine its destiny

As monarchy accedes to military

Great water systems fail
Agriculture wanes forfeiting stability
Forfeiting immunity to invasion
Portugal gains influence
As do other countries
Sri Lanka's inner divisions
Become an Achilles' heel to invaders
Great Britain colonizes the island
Ruling for over one hundred years
Yet after independence
Tamil Tigers fight the Sinhalese
Causing great massacres
Taking thousands of hostages
Peace is declared in 2009
After 100,000 killed in war
Lie now with the bones
Of millennia of peoples
SinhaleseTamil Hindu Buddhist
A veil of sadness is drawn over Sri Lanka
A dowager empress of ancient cultures
Bearing her history with pride
Yet walking softly
Over the graves of her island legends
Mourning all those
Buried now as was Bolongada
In the sands of Sri Lanka

Mindanao and Durian Fruit

Mindanao
A name that rolls off the tongue
Sultanate of Maguindanaon natives
Building on tens of thousands of years
Of civilization
Evolves into modern governance
Brought to a halt for a moment of shock
In a massacre of 58 people
November, 2009
Mostly journalists
And family of Toto Mangudatu
Filing paperwork for him to run for governor
Against Andal Ampatuan Jr.
Massacred in the town of Ampatuan
Massacred for opposing the family of Ampatuan
Mangudatu becomes governor
While still grieving his murdered wife and family
But is again threatened by Ampatuan agents
In a mall where his bodyguard defends him
And his children
Last year the murderers were convicted
Under Rodrigo Duterte
Who has allegedly killed hundreds of drug dealers
Death squads have not decreased poverty

Nor rid the lovely islands of corruption
The aftermath of Marcos
Whose opposition, Ninoy Aquino, was assassinated
Even with six years presidency by his widow Corazon
The politics of warlords
Patronage and mafia dominance
Martial law and corruption
Continue in a land defined by beauty
The largest island in a land
Of islands, flowers, glorious sunsets
Known perhaps well for its durian fruit
Large spiky and a warning to all
Delicious and yet emitting a stench
Reminiscent of the politics
Of the largest island
In the beautiful Philippines

South Sudan

Riven with conflict and poverty
Riven with discontent
Riven with discrimination
Women and children
Whose ancestors were marched
Into slavery from south Sudan
Called slaves if they are black
Called slaves by their peers
Called slaves by those who
Consider themselves Arabs
Followers of Islam
Those marched north to slavery
Want to return to their homes
In south Sudan
To their Christian churches
To their animist legends
From one poverty to another
Yet South Sudan
Is rich in oil
Rich in agriculture
Hampered only by infrastructure
And politics
Blocked from refineries in Sudan
Through terrorist labels

Blocked from trade
Forced from their own land
South Sudanese starve
In the midst of a country
Wealthy in resources
Poor only in means
And access
To its own potential
Riven still in conflict
And poverty

Sumatra

The largest crater on earth
Sits in the middle of Sumatra
Long arm cradling her sisters
Islands of Indonesia
The largest crater on earth
Womb of countless stories
Of creation and conflict
Three large goldfish
Shaded in red, black and white
Bonang Manalu of Batak culture and rituals
Swim in her depths
Chattering among themselves
Of their lives in Lake Toba
Guarding the gold of Gold Island
As Sumatra was called in Sanskrit
Born of eruptions inside an old volcano
Said to have resided in Mount Tuhaoweoba
Now called Mount Toba
Once spewing forth the mightiest
Volcanic eruption known to mankind
Leaving six hundred meters of ash
Birthing a small island in its waters from dormant magma
Pressed from the fist of the great Sumatran Fault
Birthing also its people the Bakanese

Otherwise thought to have come

4,000 years ago from the Philippines and Borneo

Who became protectors of the crater and its legends

The goldfish tell story of a lonely farmer

Who fished in rivers under Mount Tuhaoweba

Catching a strange large goldfish

Who begged him to let it go

Being a man of compassion

He let the fish go

Turning it into a beautiful princess

Who said she had been cursed as a fish

But they could marry

Only if he promised never to tell her secret

Or disasters would occur

He promised and they lived happily

Giving birth to a handsome son

Who loved to eat

Who ate everything in sight

One day he was asked to bring dinner to his father

But ate it before getting home

His father erupted like a volcano

Shouting his son was born of a fish

The boy ran crying to his mother to ask the truth

She told him to climb the highest tree on the mountain

And ran back to the river where she had met his father

Soon the whole valley was struck with lightning

Hammered with thunder
Drenched with rains
That filled the valley
As floods receded
Only the small island
Called Samosir was left
In the middle of a long elongated lake
Some legends say the princess turned again into a fish
While her husband turned into the island Samosir
Others speak of a scaly snake guarding the lake
Haunted voices calling at midnight
Lost souls of the lake
An old man sitting on the shore, perhaps the Batak King
Mythical ancestor of all Batak tribes
Visited by a tall ghost with a flat face
Seen only by the large fish of Lake Toba
Who felt the ripples of the longest earthquake in history
And the vast tsunami near Aceh
Washing the ghost with flat face
The red, black and white shaded goldfish
Singing of the old man on the shore of the lake
Called Old Grandpa or Old King
And the souls calling over the lake
Washing over countless endangered mammals
Roaming Sumatra
Drowning Sumatra

Creating more story of Sumatra
For three large goldfish
To memorialize
Under the shade of Mount Tuba
Where a boy born of fish
Once climbed the highest tree
Surviving to tell the tale
Still murmured by three great goldfish
Swimming about an island
Once called Gold Island in Sanskrit
For its hidden treasures of gold
Guarded by three large goldfish
Who still whisper its story
And worship in its sacred waters
In the palm of earth's greatest crater
In the palm holding its legends
Its secrets and its emerald beauty

Beju Gagang Indonesian spirit

Today I wept

Today I wept for my nation

I wept for its divisions

I wept that a coup could be attempted

A coup that has left

A nation in shock

A nation in grief

At death and injury

At an insurrection against democracy

At an insurrection against truth

At an insurrection against the Constitution

Against the people

Today I wept for my nation

As it still grieves

Incredulous and angry

At betrayal by its own president

And those incited to violence by his words

As its congress proceeds to endorse

Against a backdrop of attempted insurrection

Joseph Biden

As duly elected

President of the United States of America

To be inaugurated in two weeks

Into a presidency

Offering some of the greatest challenges

Ever met by a new president

Yet with a congress

Possibly ready to act

In support of justice

In support of our Constitution

In support of the people

Pro Trump Insurrection at Capitol January 6, 2021

A Chill

A chill runs through
Our nation's capital in January
The coldest month of the year
For Washington DC
As traitors throw themselves on the walls
Of our sacred congress
Climbing through the cold
Breaking windows and hearts
As they struggle to smother democracy
In the dead of winter
A chill runs through
Our nation's capital this week
As a fascist president
Demeans our immigrants
Demeans our blacks, our Hispanics
Encloses himself in his presidential cave
And takes no calls
Even Facebook denies him space
While he continues to deny
The legitimacy of an election

Aleph

We have read the Rubiyat of Omar Kayyam
If we were my mother's children
We know of the Arabian Nights
Ancient tales gathered and translated
Through the ages
We know the story of 1001 nights
Told by the princess Scheherazade to her Prince
To avoid execution
Stories and fantasy
Literacy so intertwined with Persian
And Arabic thought
That the Arabic Alphabet reflects
In its first letter Aleph
As in Hebrew
As the Greek Alpha
The Persian Farsi Alef
The depth of philosophy
Told in the 1001 Nights
Expression of eternity
Of escape and destiny
It is not 1000 nights
But 1001
And therein lies the conundrum
Of the Aleph

The never-ending beginning
Of all things
And the second letter beht
House
Alphabet
Eternal house
Of humanity
Sacred house
Built on words
Building 1001 nights
Originating in the alphabet
Shared by North Africa East Asia
All Middle Eastern peoples
One eternal expression
Growing parallel to other pictures of thought
Throughout the world
Yet resting on the aleph
Beginning of 1001 ideas
An eternity of language
In the beginning was the word
In the beginning was the aleph
Housed in beht
Housed in the sacred alphabet

Sweeping the Halls of Congress

They are sweeping the halls of congress of debris
They are sweeping our sacred portal to democracy
Of vestiges of an affront upon its integrity
Of the rags of defeat and betrayal
While he who is president still remains aloof
Aloof to his call to supporters to march
Aloof to his own promise
To join them in their march to congress
His promise to support anarchy
In the halls of democracy
While he baths his mob
In words of love
And the promise
This is just a beginning
Just a beginning to his treachery
They are sweeping the halls of congress of debris
Debris left by a mob of thugs
Obsequious sycophants to betrayal
Bowing at the throne of a satanic ruler
Caring only about himself
His golf and his tweets
His hair and his legacy of dominance
Obsequious sycophants
Bowing only to a coward

Who would not walk with them

Into the sacred temple

He targeted for insurrection

Not for fear of blasphemy

Not for honor of its glory

Not out of respect for history

But out of cowardice alone

They are sweeping the halls of congress for debris

Sweeping the halls of the rags of failure

To cleanse it of its emperor

The emperor with no clothes

Wearing only a mantel of deceit and arrogance

Rocks

Climbing over shoreline rocks

I wonder at their history

Their origins

Were they washed to the shore

By ocean waves and wind

Or tumbled from slides down a mountain

Or spewed from inland springs

They seem not to care

If they come from there or where

Yet lightly perch or seem to stay

Impervious to weather

Decorated with mussels

Or cradling crabs and tiny life

Rife with unique form and purpose

Sentinels of stone as landmarks

Offering footholds for small feet

To climb and meet seaweed and foam

Observe the ocean's home

Rattling from their rocky dome

Intrepid waves obeying laws

A child can scarcely comprehend

Yet bends her body to the tide

In awe of rocks that still defy

The ocean's power sweeping by

Someone said to me

All the thugs under Trump's thumb
Will scramble quickly one by one
Under a rug or shoe or rock
From which they came in disarray
To undermine ethics and law
Obeying one demagogic call
To racism and fascist power
Over Hispanic black or native
Immigrant or refugee
Those seeking refuge at our borders
Those seeking it through law and order
Based on human rights ensconced
In international decrees and charters
The rock or rug or shoe hides those
Who scramble hands and feet and toes
As their tyrant is disabused of his visions of fascist glory
And yet they wait to rise anew
When yet another comes in view
To thread another fascist story
Told for his own fascist glory
Freedom lovers watch those rocks
And shoes and rugs and ticking clocks
Who wait until their time is come
To rise again tick tock tick tock

Cleaning Up

A foggy San Francisco
Peeks out from her foggy blanket
Unsure if she is welcome
In a brand new world
Feeling compromised
By her own nation
Disabused of faith in law
Yet hearing coastal winds of freedom
Whisper that blue skies are gathered
Behind foggy mists of question
Truth is hiding
Ready to emerge
Just vacuuming the skies
Of vestiges of hate
Vestiges of betrayal
Vestiges of lies
Cleaning up
For a new day

Cave Son Doong

There is an enormous cave

Four million years old

In an area of Vietnam

Born 400 million years ago

A cave of 90 meter long stalactites

Of crushed roofs

Allowing sunlight and rainforests to thrive

Inside its enormity

Rivers flowing through

Birds indigenous to its walls and native trees

Singing its story of the ages

Hiding away an enormous eco-library of millennia

Found by a Vietnamese farmer

Who lost his way in the forest

And could not find his way back

To the hidden cave for years

Until he stumbled again on

The gaping maw of Hang Son Doong

Offering its gigantic old

Wrinkled, scarred mouth

Tattooed and sculptured

Millions of millennia long

By tools of nature

Light and wind and water

Seismic arms
Primeval chatter
Yet reaching through those arms
The farmer found light
Weaving through chaos
Weaving through darkness
Weaving through confusion
Underground illumination

A Frigid Cave

The coldest part of the universe
Nearly two billion light years long
Photons moving up and down
An icy hill
Sliding more slowly down
Applying the brakes
As its waves grow longer
Becoming colder and colder
Moving slower and slower
A frigid desert in the universe
Nearly a void
Yet containing bits of matter
Stellar, planetary, dark galaxies
Swirling within the largest structure
Of our universe
Expanding and shrinking
Enormous bellows
Within a sunken hole
Of cosmic rock
A vast cave of anti-plasma
Vacuuming and spewing
Gravitational energy
Gigantic lungs
Of dark balance

...and they'll come home
(Enigma of compatibility and relationships)

Sheep are still astray
After Christmas Day
The shepherdess has
Called
Bo Peep has lost her sheep
One called comp
Another pa
One hid under her table
Yet many moons they
Strayed till Bo Peep
Doubted she was able
To ever call them back
To scrub their wool
Or write their fable
She even called a counselor
To ask what was amiss
And why her sheep would
Go astray
She really could not guess
But thought perhaps she was not meant
To be Bo Peep at all
And put away her bonnet
Ate her curds and whey and pondered
And wondered why she lost her sheep
She just could not recall
Through spring and summer came again
And even leaves of fall
Day faded slowly into day
Her sheep were gone
That's all

Cracks, Rags and Watercolors

There is a crack in the sky
Evening clouds crowd in
Leaving soft light
Auguring a moment of thought
Before the crack is closed
And evening settles softly
There is a crack in the sky
As clouds move slowly
While birds soar against the dying light
Windows become bright squares
Against a ceding sunset
Gray sky rests in rags
Somber watercolor wash
Peering down on cities
Considering the closing crack
In their moving ceiling
Wondering if social cracks
Might also be washed away
With watercolors
A paintbrush of politics
Sweeping justice
Through the clouds of congress

Metal Detectors for Lawmakers

We now have metal detectors

Through which congresspersons must pass

To enter their Capitol for debate

Post 2021 insurrection

One wonders if they will allow such checks

Or if pandemic protections

Distancing and masks

Might make such passages problematic

Whether those who think themselves elite

Might sidestep such restraints

Whether guns might make their way

Into the house or senate

Unseen and undetected

Whether the eastern seat of power

Might find itself a new wild west

A high noon moment

Oblivious of all restraints

To enter a sacred space

Now stained with blood

Baby Magnetar

A baby magnetar
Only five hundred years old
Spins in her cradle
Faster than you can imagine
Faster than one and a half seconds
Every revolution
No time to burp
Breathing pulsars so quickly
She has no time to flee
To send debris
Or even turn her spins
Into x rays as magnetars do
Born of collapsed stars
She snuggles in our Milky Way
Content to be the baby
With only thirty sibling magnetars
Happy to gurgle radio waves
To smiling telescopes
Bending over her cradle
A very tiny neutron star
Who lost her mother super nova
Somewhere during her birth
Yet was discovered
By earthling admirers

About the time they had to lockdown

Due to a plague

And found her spinning

In her milky nursery

21,000 light years away

Smiling to a welcoming

Universe

Just learning to babble

Stardust

A Small Red House

A long, narrow pier leads to a small red house

In the middle of an unnamed lake

In the middle of an unnamed country

Beckoning me to walk there

And knock on the door

And yet strangely telling me

It wants to be left alone

Tempting yet unwelcoming

Like the gingerbread house

In Hansel and Gretel

Inhabited by a witch

Collecting children

The idea making me shiver

Yet unbelieving of such stories

I walk by the narrow pier

With its small red house

Double masked

On my solitary way home

To my own space

Unwelcoming to others

Because of a seemingly endless pandemic

Wondering still

About solitary houses

At the end of long piers

In the middle of romantic lakes

In the middle of unnamed countries

In the middle of a pandemic

In the middle of an unwelcoming society

Unwelcoming to all who cannot sustain themselves

Unwelcoming to all who come from somewhere else

Unwelcoming to all who seem different

Unwelcoming to the other one

Unwelcoming even in my dreams

Where a small red house

At the end of a long pier

Remains tempting

Like a gingerbread house

Yet closed

Impervious to touch

Impervious to its own story

Impervious to a knock

From a stranger

Someone different

Other

Impervious

To the thought of a long journey

On a long pier

Walked by a stranger

Knocking

On its closed red door

Light Whispering

Bars of light flung by Venetian blinds
Sliced by shadow
Creating triangles of light upon the floor
Rectangles flung upon a wall and window
Geometry run amok
Light reflecting spots of dust
Seeming to give voice in sounds of birds
Finches chorusing lightly
From trees and eaves
Square things
Roof shadows
Games of sunshine
Moving beyond my blinds
To dance in song and shadow
Light whispering
Among its shadows

Metamorphosis of Cloud

An arm reaches across the sky
White and soft
With ragged edges
Reaching somewhere unknown
Disintegrating as the day wanes
Elusive fingers
Unable to grasp
The light of sunset
Or the song of birds
Intangible spirit softness
Reaching towards nothing
Gradually retreating while
Opening to blue
Yet still reaching
In gray tones
As darkness fills the sky
Long arm of cloud
Reaches across the sky
Alone, stretching
Knowing its time is short
That it will stretch and dissipate
Like dreams

Finding Tomorrow

We re-invent tomorrow

Picking up the pieces of today

Gently washing off the stains of yesterday

Softly scrubbing rags of hope

To place them on a clothesline hung with sunshine

We all re-invent tomorrow

Shadowed by betrayal

Dripping wet upon our consciousness

Clearing space for new beginnings

Walking among ruins and debris

Carefully avoiding unmasked strangers

Knowing we must re-invent together

While walking under wrung out thoughts

Once redolent with greed and hate

Now dripping into streets of fate-marked

Corners bleeding unmarked signs

Directionless we wander

Sodden streets auguring springtime

Sudden pulsing of new sprouts

Pushing through damp ever

Determined to regenerate again

Indomitable nature re-invents

As if there never were a need

To seek tomorrow

Not Yet Finished Moon

Last night the sky blushed
Pink and coral
Spreading lightly
Cheeks blushing from the west
To the bowl of heaven
Within her blush a lightly sketched
Waxing crescent moon
Floated like a lost gondola
Knowing she had just been
Painted onto the sky
And was not yet finished

Petra

Caves, temples, tombs
A honeycomb of blushing stone
Often called Rose City
Rests in ruins close to the port of Aqaba
At the top of the Red sea in Jordan
Where double arms reach into the Sinai
Shallow Gulf of Suez invites a canal
To the Mediterranean
Deep Gulf of Aqaba invites ships
From the vast Indian Ocean
Passing Gulf of Aden
Welcoming visitors from Asia and Africa
From Europe and beyond
Some seeking Sinai to the Mediterranean
Some seeking the honeycomb of Petra
Built over two thousand years ago
Hidden in sand for centuries
Now gradually showing her face
While continuing excavations
Sing of her past beauty
Her present glory vulnerable to new scars
Hammered on her flesh with bombs
Yet she still tempts
With harmonious structures dedicated to Dushara

And the Nabatean gods
Yet welcoming to gods of Greek and Romans
To Jew and Arab
To those whose history began with Abraham
Once home to shared ideas and hopes
She still tempts visitors
To revel at her countenance
Her temples stretched on summits of rugged mountains
Her elegant silk tomb
Her Byzantine cathedral
Testimony to her embrace of all peoples
Thriving from trade of spice and incense
And countless springs of water
And underground cisterns
Hiding within her network of stones
And roughhewn foundations
Painted with ephemeral tones
Changing with the hours of the sun
She is like a goddess
Once veiled with the sand of the desert
Now gazing on a temporal world
Whose camel caravans
Still testify to her longevity and grace
Nibbling at her grasses
Plodding slowly by her gates
As she ponders new ideas

Jehudah Halevi

Born in Toledo or Tudela
Ruled by a Muslim dynasty
Embracing continual dialogue
Of Muslim Christian and Jew
Hellenic philosophy and science
Halevi absorbed universality in poetry
Was recognized in Cordoba
Invited to Granada by the great poet Ezra
And thrived until Ezra his patron was murdered
Giving him his first lesson in distrust
His lesson in racism and otherness
Pushing him away from the universal
To absorb his own Jewishness
As the root of his poetry
His tree of many limbs
Climbed by Aristotle, Abraham, Moses, Jesus
His tree of science, intuition and logic
Demanding inclusion
Yet knowing life excludes
Racism and otherism nibble at his tree
Of the knowledge of good and evil
His tree of philosophy religion and science
Inspiring his greatest poem
His Khusari

Of a king of the Khusars who dreams
Dreams dreams of a god
Dreams dreams of a god who loves and scolds
Dreams dreams of a god
Who admires his thinking admonishes his inaction
Demands he seek his roots
Pushing him to seek Jerusalem
The heart of his tree of universalism
A medieval journey into his past
A medieval journey into ideas
To seek his roots
And mark a journey from body to head
A journey of his body in the west to his soul in the east
As we must all journey to the roots of our soul
The roots of a universal tree
To find the fibers running under each tree
Connecting us all to the spirit of the forest
The spirit of revelation
So Halevi subsumes his own poetry
Subsumes his message of god to the king
As his own call to journey from west to east
As his own journey
To Jerusalem to find his soul
Where he finds death
Some say under the trampling hooves of camels
Oblivious of the exhausted poet

In the city of Jerusalem

Death in a forest of belief

At the root of his heart

Death as the beginning of a journey

The beginning of a journey

To the root of his soul

Odyssey of Carménère

It was in the late eighties
I left our vineyards in Guenoc Valley
To fly to France
To find Carménère
Sometimes called Grand Vidure
The temperamental Bordeaux grape
Not yet legal for import to our country
Rich in intensity
Yet often subject to coulure
Difficult to fertilize
Tending to shatter
Making multi-sized grapes
Loved and hated by winegrowers
Yet perhaps the most noble of the Bordeaux family
Ancient and venerable
Beloved by the great enologist
Louis Pierre Pradier
Whom I met at his vineyard
At 8:30 in the evening on a summer night
Exactly twelve hours late
Due to flight and train delays
Yet reaching him immediately at his phone
Where he was waiting all day
And took me to the vineyards

Still full of light in the summer evening
To see the beautiful Carménère
Ripening on the vines
And taste its tiny fruits
Took me to his laboratory
Where he was growing a vine hybrid
Of Petit Verdot and Carménère
Passionate as was I about Carménère
And its cousin Petit Verdot
And then to his tiny personal cellar
Where he asked if I would prefer to take a bottle
Or taste with him
I hoped for both and he offered me a taste
From an unmarked bottle
I immediately smelled the aroma and tasted the juice
Exclaiming this is like the Petit Verdot we grow at home!
To which Louis Pierre Pradier replied
Yes, it is Petit Verdot
Now let us taste the Carménère
Which proved deeply intense deeply complex
Blackberry, coffee, briary tones and wild cherry
Notes of eucalyptus and thyme
A veritable banquet of fruits and spices
Ethereal unfamiliar herbal notes
Unearthly packed orchestra of fruit
Rich on the palate

An unending finish

Carménère

Fairer than fair

Worthy of a longer journey

Which it then took to come to the United States

Fifty tests for purity in Geneva New York

And in Saahnichten on Vancouver Island in Canada

Where I visited Louis Pierre Pradier again and

His laboratory of Carménère

Suffering years of tests and evaluation

Finally receiving certification for export to America

Export to Oregon

To be cloned sufficiently for planting

I saw the hydroponic cloning

A multitude of vines like babies in a nursery

Climbing into history

A new history in America

Where Carménère

Now enriches the great wines from Bordeaux and Medoc

Cabernet Sauvignon, Merlot, Cabernet Franc, Malbec

Carménère

Grown in California and beyond

Grown in Chile even before

But with its their birth certificate in Bordeaux

Nurtured in the Blanquefort laboratory

Of Louis Pierre Pradier

Named the Guenoc-Melander Carménère Clone

Much to my dismay

But then my honor

Recognizing the long journey

Of a princess to our country

Fairest of the fair

The princess Carménère

Together

We are met on a great battlefield
Martyrs to truth spread about us
Ideas held hostage
While a new leader
Holds the mantel of hope
Holds the mantel of compassion
Holds us waiting
Upon that battlefield
Still strewn with relics of battle
Still strewn with brokenness
Waiting to be healed
An eagle calls in the distance
Reminding us of courage
Reminding us to fly together
To place our destiny in each other
To lean on those we would support
To embrace each other
As we reach out to the world
As we stretch our arms and hands
To every nation every creed every color
We stretch our wings into a future
Worthy of the eagles' flight
Reaching back to those who want to fly
But need more strength

Reaching back to those who are unsure
Reluctant
Fledgling spirits of democracy
Needing to be nurtured
Assured that we will fly together
Unsure of our destiny
Unsure of our destination
But knowing the journey
To a promised land of justice
Somewhere over a near horizon
Is one we must make
Together

Algeria

Gateway between Africa and Europe

Mediterranean Algeria

Hominid Neolithic Artistic past

Leaving great cave paintings

In Tassiri-n-Ajjer

Great ruins from Roman empires

Farmers hunters believers

Berber poets without written language

Watched Phoenicians build their Carthage

Waited for Romans to dismantle it

Berbers enslaved as soldiers

Paid tribute to Carthage

Yet traded with both Carthage and with Rome

Watching them fight their Punic wars

Waited and created their own kingdoms

In their fertile hinterland

Becoming indispensable to Rome

When Carthage tumbled into ruins

Berbers remained

Indispensable granary of the Roman Empire

Annexing themselves to Rome

Adopting Christianity

Expedient perhaps

Or preferable to war

Yet Islam came with Arab Umayyads
Converting Berbers to their faith and power
Claiming and converting all North Africa
Then ceding that domain to Abbasids
Who ruled from Baghdad as a caliphate
Manifesting art and learning
Its Rustumid imams becoming famous
For great scholarship, honesty, piety, justice
Yet losing balance in peaceful pursuits
Neglecting military
Having no standing army
Victims to the Fatimids' great military
Who conquered and departed
Wanting only conquest of Egypt and beyond
Leaving Algeria to its Berbers
Who then fell in awe to Arab Bedouins
Great in number and ideas
Conquering hearts and minds of desert people
To Arabic language and vision
Yet Sanhaja Berbers of Western Sahara
Turned the spirit of religion into military strength
Conquering Morocco and all of the land
From the Mediterranean to Spain's Ebro River
Reminted as Almohad
Yet far too vast to govern
Enduring inner strife until the Ottomans took control

Spain bringing Christianity when it conquered Granada
Yet loved to build castles more than govern
And Ottomans found profit in privateering
Making Red Beard Barbarossa famous
Sultans and pashas ruled the land
Turkish supremacy taught discrimination
Against Arabs and Berbers
Racism extending its mood and manner
Till a new pasha took power over Algeria
Absolving Ottomans of need to govern a disparate land
Prey to Napoleon yet rich in trade with Europe
Algeria was soon at war again
Even America made war
Upon the Barbary States
War and tribute
Trade and strife
Mark Algeria's history
A pawn in France's deep desire to own her land
For shipping, farming, settlement
Torn apart for years
A million dying in wars with France
Till independence sends Algeria's settlers
Her colons, her Blackfeet
Fearful of retribution
Back to France
Leaving behind a land of sand and coastal beauty

Rubbing cheeks with Mali Mauritania Niger Tunesia Libya
Sitting on rich oil and gas reserves
Hiding beneath her vast desert sands
Nurturing an ancient Berber people
Unsure she can trust her presidents
Unsure she can trust the world about her
Sure only of the eternal sea
Washing up upon her fertile northern coast
Washing up on glorious ruins of Hellenic history
As she kneels upon her vast expanse of sand
Arms stretched to Africa and Europe
Nodding to the sky and sun
Knowing she remains as one
Algeria

Pain and Kindness

1.

A boy could not talk

He had lost everything

Had been abused

Yet sat with other boys

In a church in safety

Listening to We Shall Overcome

Sung by boys who accepted him

And his speechlessness

He opened his mouth and sang

We shall overcome

And all could finally hear

His voice

2

Soldiers took little children

As hostages

In Sri Lanka

Their mothers came

Speaking of understanding

The trauma of soldiers

But asked to have their children back

Asked the soldiers for their children

Who were released to them

With fear but sorrow

Fear of repercussions
But even greater sorrow
At pain they had caused
Pain to the children
Pain to the mothers
Pain to themselves

3
A ball is taken from a child
By another child
Who covets all balls
And hides them
Saying "mine"
The child whose ball was taken
Offers the taking child
A truck as well
The taking child
Gives back the ball
And both of them play
One taught
One learning
The beauty of kindness

Natural Friends

The tree sends roots beneath the stream
Where beavers choose to build
A home of sticks and weeds and dreams
And soon with beaver children filled
Who quickly sully her clear waters
Yet she thinks of them
Quite simply as her sons and daughters
Living in a dam
Although they chew and paw and scrape
Upon her roots and bark
Break off her limbs for their small home
Like playing in a park
She smiles serenely far above
The stream and beavers' home
Watches fish who come to play
Where they can safely roam
Where beavers make a dam of sticks
A dam for fish to thrive
While beaver children fish and friends
Live happily inside
And far above the tree smiles down
And stretches out and bends
And showers leaves and acorns
Down upon her little friends

Rainbow Diva

On the road to Hana in Maui
A rainbow grows
Throwing bark
Like shedding garments
In the jungle
Bit by bit
Light and dark
Each garment shredding
Her nude body
From a naughty rainbow mesh
As a strip tease of the jungle
Shows her eucalyptus flesh
Naked demoiselle of Maui
Proudly carries her straight limbs
Noble emerald and blue dowry
Hues of gold and copper pence
Dressed as queen of green Hawaii
Tempting elegant eloquence
Carried once from Mindanao
Where her sister still enchants
Shedding veils of parchment garments
In her eucalyptus dance

A Moon Moment

A half-moon sailed last night
Over a gold and blushing sunset
Her waxing silver tossed so high
It seemed almost to leave a sky
Of fading blue to rue its distance
From a sunset's bold display
Of rosy light bedding the day

An Unacknowledged Miracle

Today I walked under an almost gibbous moon
Half hidden by ragged clouds
Vestiges of yesterday's rainstorm
Dancing with a freshly washed sun
Smiling down on glistening trees
Her light creating blue yet luminous sky
Today I walked under choruses of birdsong
Finch and warbler chirps
A descant to the sparrows' virtuoso
Leaps and trills betraying her assumed humility
Pigeons' cooing pedal marking time
Today I climbed upon a dampened hill
Footsteps crushing sodden leaves
Rocks dislodged and bumping elbows as they rolled
While rags of clouds and sodden leaves
Conspired to frame a dampened day
Under pale moon and rain-washed sun
Both witness and protagonist
To just another unacknowledged miracle

Navalny Waits

Alexey Navalny stands in Novosibirsk
Great Russian university city
In the Siberian forest
To speak of corruption in Moscow
To speak of stacked political cronies
Keeping Putin in power
On his return from Siberia
Flying over the massive Siberian forest
Navalny takes ill
Needing a ventilator
As he flies over the lungs of the world
Bottles of water in his hotel room
Test positive for traces of poison
Traces of Novichoc
Fearful of Russian doctors
Navalny is rushed to Berlin
Treated there for five months
For suspected poisoning
Returns to Moscow
Unafraid of repercussions
For his demand for reform
For his message of corruption
Exposed egregiously with his own arrest
On charges the international court

Deems illegitimate

Fifteen thousand protest his detention

Over three thousand are arrested

Navalny waits

He waits for justice

As do others

Wrapped into a decaying system

Once KGB now GRU and ISD

A spy system

Once humiliated by the landing of Matthias Rust

In his Cessna on Moscow Square

Embarrassed again as Bellingcat finds

Three hundred five secret agents

Simply by fumbled car registrations

The Skripal poisoning failure mocks the world

Betrayals and unmasking of spies continues

Puten's own machinations exposed

His empire questioned

Like dolls within dolls of Russian toys

All roll out like pieces of a broken puzzle

So does Russia's spy puzzle

Like Humpty Dumpty

Fail to put itself together again

Awakening

The air is chill
The moon was waxing
Still afloat in afterthought
As morning breaks
Birds whisper against cool air
Discussing whether they should get up
And leave their downy nests
Their holes in naked trunks of
Sturdy tree apartments
Perched on the cusp of dawn
Their small bodies drowsy with remnants of the night
Emerging sun with arms of silver light
Stretching to gold
Reaching into crevices of nests and trees
Caressing feathers kissing eyelids
Opening like tiny shutters to the day
Infinitesimal screens sliding back
And hiding into secret chambers
While their hosts flutter
As they putter through assorted leaves
Seeking breakfast in the trees

I Walk with Shadows

I walk along a garden path
My shadow guiding me
While tiny shadows flicker past
Reminding me of family
The wind makes shades of leaves
Dancing brightly underneath
Beside my shadowed feet
While bird song seems to strum
A whispered descant to
My muffled beat
Treading a path of birds and bees
And trees and leaves and squirrels and me
And all things breathing on my path
Breathing together on my path
My shadow family

Another Day

The curtain opens slowly
Question of blue remains bare
Sparing thoughts of cloud
Waiting in the wings
Bringing memories of rain
Draining still in treasuries
Of water sullied fully
Deep in gullies streaming
To the arms of oceans
Beds of rivers
Tributaries taking dully
Sullied water to its plankton
Marine creatures
Nesting algae
Thoughts of fish
In trenches full of plastic
Waiting duly in the pits
An orchestra of strings
Sonic vibrations in the wings
Of nature's stage
The curtain trembles
Ropes unfurled
While sun and moon
Contest the roles played

On a living breathing stage

Of time and season

Rain and reason

Pouring into another day

The Rugged Road to Hana

On the rugged road to Hana
Hidden waterfalls sing songs
Feathered songbirds throng the jungle
Giant ferns embrace the ground
On the rugged road to Hana
Every curve a secret charm
Like the body of a woman
Curled into an island's arm
Reaching out to hold you captive
With her rustling perfumed breeze
Beckoning gently with her whisper
Blowing scents among palm trees
On the rugged road to Hana
Fabled stories chatter streams
Sacred pools await your coming
In the Hana of your dreams

I Am Sure

I am sure fairies walk along the path
Cast by the dying sun over ocean waves
I am sure dolphins whisper secrets
Diving under fairy feet
I am sure that stars are beckoned
To accompany the dusk
And give cadence to the moonlight
Shining on the fairy path
I am sure the night is magic
When your breath matches my sighs
And the Pleiades all whisper
When the moon becomes your eyes

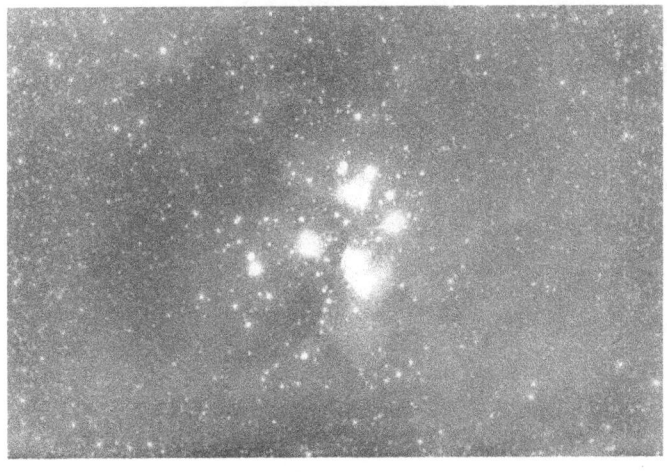

Love and Nature

I can't imagine love without nature
Rustling trees picnics in sunshine
Falling in love on old Cape Cod
Moonlight kisses
Melting in the morning sun
Cars parked under the stars
A winding stream
Which comes first
Nature or love
You are the promised kiss of springtime
The only pretty ringtime
When birds do sing
Hey ding a ding ding ring a ding ding
Sweet lovers love the spring
I want to snuggle with my love
Into Pandora's box of nature
Where demons have been banished
And hope remains
With trees and streams and rocks
And my love
Holding me tight
Under a beautiful tree
In a field of flowers
In the moonlight

Rock of our Nation

As with every boulder
So is our nation
Intrepid rock of generations
Worn away by time
By children climbing on her face
Rivers challenging her valor
Trees and creatures in her shadow
Wearing down her cracks and crannies
Yet creating something new
Nascent sprouting of new springtimes
Nascent learning of new songs
Each surge bringing new beginnings
Evolution of ideas
Rocky boulder
You our nation
Hewn in blood and pain and wisdom
Shall endure the life and river
Shall live its surge and power
Shall become its life and spirit
Shall renew us all again

Wings to Forever

I walk with my love

Keeping the distance of forever

Sheltering in place

Where there is no place

Walking in shadows

Amorphous

Spiritual

Pieces of existence

Found only in dreams

Watching the wind

Blowing leaves

Becoming wings

To forever

Only Questions

Once I thought
He wanted me to try to love again
How can one slide out of arms
Lost in death
To find another
To embrace a different warmth
A new skin
Like peeling off one's own soul
To stand more than nude
Lost vulnerable alone
In a strange embrace
Signifying
Only questions

Spring Survives

Finches trill in the cool morning
Gulls fly over the city streets
Curious about dry lands, buildings and hills
Dogs patrol the streets on leashes
A strange silence reigns
Butterflies appear
Surprised at their own wings
Hibernating nature
Pokes her nose into the sunshine
Spring survives
Even a pandemic

Morning Moon

The moon this morning
Pale gibbous moon
With ragged edges
Peeking into cool dawn light
Timidly wondering
If she had forgotten to exit
Yet a welcome sight to me
Needing company
On a cool solitary morning
Remembering a large warm round moon
Filling my window in another place
Another time
When it was our window
Our moon
Our love

Shadowless

Crowd cover erases shadows
In the early afternoon
Dismissing the light of sunshine
Trying desperately to pierce
Through darkening clouds

Home in a Closed World

What is home in a closed world?
Closed to protect frail humankind
Against a mysterious virus
I walk outside and feel I am home
Air and rain clouds and sunshine
Nature's hands and face
Wind racing to catch my hat
Hot air against my mask
I wear to protect the joggers
Who run by on the sidewalk
While I detour into the street
Home is where my heart is
My heart is everywhere
Wondering where to go
In a closed world
Imagining a fresh planet
An earth mother
An earth family
Whose voice is the birds
Whose face is the clouds
Whose hands offer wind and rain
Lift up the sun in the morning
And the moon at night
And paint the glorious sunrise and sunset

For the wallpaper of my true home

My family of nature

I hear her voice chattering

A symphony of birdsong

A chorus of sea lions

A descant of raindrops and singing wind

An embrace of fog and sunbeams

And I am home

Nevermore

The moon is full and wanders through the sky
Casting over earth her golden eye
Rolling upon silk bereft of stars
She reigns supreme and waits in space for Mars
How eloquent the patient moon remains
The partner she awaits still red with war
While she prepares her offerings of peace
And hears the raven speaking, "Nevermore"

Oh moon, how difficult your role becomes
Pulled by the tides to glow on their own blue
Yet following a path you do not choose
A journey on a sky you must cross through
To seek to light the sky with perfect grace
Inspiring tenderness in love's embrace
Your scared roundness bathes the world in light
As you become our vision in the night

Slaughter of Innocents in Newtown

December, 2012

Let us name the names

Of children

Let us name the names

Of lighted candles

Snuffed out by a violent wind of rage

A soul on fire and pitiless

Destroying sweetness

Let us name the names

Ana, Jesse, Charlotte, James, Grace, Emilie, Anna, Benjamin, Olivia, Chase, Catherine, Jack, Jessica, Avielle, Daniel, Dylan, Josephine, Madeline, Noah, Allison, Catherine, Violet

Let us name the names

Of children

Shot not once

But twice

Each shot twice

Their laughter silenced

Their tears still wet and mixed with blood

Their voices muted

Tiny bodies torn

Let us mourn the children

Let us name the names

Of children

Six and seven years old

Full of life and love

Full of tomorrow

Let us name their names

Wrenched with anguish

We

Wanting all of it to be a dream

A jagged metaphor gone wrong

Wanting to

Reset the computer

Run the film back to

Living laughter, happy smiles, eyes of hope

Reset the computer on Friday, December 14

To an earlier moment

Restore the lives of children

The lives of their brave teachers

Trying in vain to shield them

In the rain of bullets

Let us name the names of children

But let us not forget

The massacre of innocents

Everywhere

Let us not forget our own shame

The blood on our hands

The slaughter of innocents

The names upon names

Of children

Mohammed, Said, Abdullah, Hassan, Dunya

Shot or bombed

Killed or maimed

Reset the computers of the world

To a day of peace

Set them back

And farther back

Set them back

Set them back

Set them back

To a day when

This country

One day did not make war

Did not send drones which killed children

Did not incarcerate innocents

In prisons

Did not kill

Did not render children and their parents

To torture and death

Did not set an example

Of violence and bullying to all the world

Reset the computers and clocks

Set them back

Till we may never

Need to

Name other names

Never need to name the names

Of children

We have killed

Fame

Min Yongjin

Stabbed 23 children

In Chenpeng

So he could get on TV

Before the end of the world

The Iron Road (Railroad memories)

The Iron Road

Still extant

Beckons travelers

To walk its historic route

Whistles steam creaking joints

Locomotive blasts and chugs

Resonant memories

Lonely people riding the rails

To fatal encounters

Or movie star fame

Hold ups

Wild horses racing

Racing the iron horse

Racing into history

Tracks extend from nowhere

Into everywhere

Tracks for presidents

Tracks for milk runs

Tracks for trekking

Trekking

Beckoning

Travelers

From here

To there

Into memories

Of Chinese laborers

Hammering

Sweating

Dying

For a railroad

Hanging in baskets

Woven with their own hands

Let down

Drawn up

Sometimes destroyed

By the explosives

They had set below

Rocking in their woven cradles

Or plunging from cliffs

Ten thousand Chinese

Ten thousand Dutch, Irish

Germans, Czechoslovakian

Immigrants, veterans

Twenty thousand

Working on the railroad

Working as slaves for

Judah, the founder

Financed by

The Big Four

Huntington, Stanford, Hopkins, Crocker

Under the corrupt hands of

Thomas Durant

Saved only by Grenville Dodge

Engineer of railroads

Civil War railroads

Famous for leaving

No track of his whereabouts

Except for the

Wooden trails

Now trailing

From Sacramento to Utah

Forced to join the eastern track

At Promontory Point

Salt Lake

Tears sweat and anguish

Death and greed

The heroism of immigrants

Forging the golden spike

That joined the Iron Road

Old trail of pioneers

Trail of native tribes

Trail of immigrants

Rails of iron

Forged on wood

Forged with blood

Forged with tears

Now memories

Containing ghosts that beckon

Beckon travelers

To walk with them

Walk with them

Along the iron road

The Moon was Hiding

The moon was hiding

In the sunset tonight

Just a thin bright circle

Floating there

As if devouring

Orange cotton candy

Sticky candy

Melting on its cheeks

Dissolving slowly

Into the evening sky

Knowing Where You Are

When journalist John McPhee wrote of Bill Bradley
Basketball player Princeton
Who could ring a basket from anywhere on the court
Without seeming to see the basket
How he did it
Bill replied you have to have a sense of where you are
It takes time work practice commitment love
As with anything if you are to find your way
As with life when you think you are lost
Find a sense of where you are on the journey
Be centered work practice commit love
Pay attention
Make amends
Be generous
Know your teammates
Forget yourself as you center on
Where you are
Your purpose your soul wrapped and sewn in kindness
Thrown from anywhere
On the basketball court of life
Will find itself
And where you are

Cyrus the Great of Persia

Cyrus
Student of Socrates
Known for his conquest of Babylon
For founding the Persian monarchy
Based the first human rights charter
On his Cyrus Cylinder
Created 2,600 years ago
Proclaiming linguistic, racial and religious equality
Freeing slaves to return home to rebuild their lands
To rebuild their lives
Freeing the Jews in Babylon
To return to Jerusalem
And rebuild their temples
Thomas Jefferson made his sons
Read the cylinder
After they had learned Greek
President Harry Truman is said to have claimed
"I am Cyrus"
Our Iranian legacy is democracy
Feeding its ideas into our Constitution
Iran celebrated the 2,500th Anniversary of the Cylinder
And the founding of the Persian Empire

With a gift of the replica of the Cylinder

To the United Nations in 1971

Iroquois and Persians

Thousands of years ago

Created societies of equality and justice

As modern nations still seek to emulate

Still seek better to implement

Great ideas and laws

Inherent to free societies

Yet still stumble

On paths to justice

Cyrus Cylinder, British Museum

Prison to Punish

Prison

Cage

No exit

Words of terror

Anathema to human existence

Assumed necessary

For those who have abused social norms

Abused others

Killed, injured, robbed, slandered

Taken or sold drugs

Prison

Prisoner

Less than human

Once a prisoner

Always a prisoner

Afraid

Afraid of shadows

Afraid of friends

Afraid

Or angry

Afraid

Or full of hatred

Freed

Yet full of memories

Of prison

Inhuman, unforgiving

Made to punish

Not to heal

It was not always so

Indigenous peoples

Saw social error

As a chance to begin again

To bind again

Social ideas

Families

Friends

Sought to embrace

And forgive

All animals steal

Murder for jealousy

Or anger

Territory

Or tyranny

The cuckoo bird sits upon another's nest

To hatch her egg among the sparrows

Another abandons its eggs

To seek another mate

Or freedom

And yet we do not know

Animals who torture one another

Who lock their neighbors in cages
For decades on end
For retribution
For vengeance
Not for education
Prisons do not educate
Except to teach the prisoner
To continue to repudiate
To continue to hate
To continue to seek
Asocial avenues
Out of poverty
Asocial avenues
To perceived power
Prisons do not heal
But create sickness
Prisons placate only those
Who praise retribution
Or find wealth in making prisons
Find power in having prisons
Prisons placate only those
Who do not think
To reframe all the cages
Reframe the idea of prisons
To make of prison an oasis
For those who need healing

Make of prison a garden

Where we may nurture justice

Where we may recognize ourselves

In the oasis

And seek restoration

Healing

Freedom

And release

From

The prison

That divides us

The prison

That fails to heal

The prison

That incarcerates

Our own souls

The prison

That separates

Our own souls

That separates

Those same souls

From justice

Regard (Colette, a musical by the author)

Regard! Look!

Don't just look, but see

See the sky, see the clouds

See the footprints of gods

Walking through the air

Watch the tickling fingers of treetops

Wisteria, tendrils of green

Climbing blossoms

Now seen bursting everywhere!

Bursting everywhere!

Regard! Look!

Don't just look, but dream

Dream in patterns of sunsets

Tatters of grasses

Smatters of sun etched with rainbows

Undone by the golden rays

Dream the day away

Silently away, silently away!

Regard! Look!

Don't just look, but watch!

Watch the kittens prowl

As their mothers growl

In pretended rage

Watch the spiders spin

As the days begin

To prepare the stage

Of another day

Of another day

Regard!

Tikkun

Peace
Repair the world
Repair generations
Repair severed bonds with earth
Healing
Knitting bones together
Knitting destinies with living needles
Clicking
The sound of woodpeckers
And crickets
Tapestry of sound
Woven carpets
Knitted sweaters upon trees
Waiting for snow
Bandages of whiteness cover wounds
Bleeding from an excess
Of extermination
Knitters, weavers
Singers, dancers
Curl into snows
Of healing
Waiting for
Stars to burn through

Ides

A full moon
Fifteenth or thirteenth day
But full of light
At evening
I wait quietly
For the moon
To display itself
To bless the month with cool glory
The beginning of the Roman New Year
Once celebrated with joy
Then remembered for betrayal
But it is dark
Ides of March
Et tu Brutus
Betrayal of the skies
Waiting for the moon
Neutral
Pale
The moon
Rises and slips
Inside the urn of cloud
Darkness resides
Ides

Her Hair

Her father asked me not to touch his hair
I do not dare touch his daughter's hair
My daughter
Beautiful, soft hair
Framing a lovely face
Blue eyes
She says she does not like the color blue
But her beautiful blue eyes shine
Soft and vulnerable
Sometimes faded with hurt
Veiled to protect
Against the brilliance
Of her intellect
Hidden
Under
Soft, curly tresses of her thick, luxuriant hair
Sometimes painful for her as a child
When I brushed it
Trying to be careful
Mother, why do you talk about my hair?
What don't you like about it?
It is beautiful
I love the way it frames your face
Oh

The Fog Settles

The fog

Settles

Under the moon

Dampening

City streets

I walk slowly

In a

Cloud

As a Child I Walked

As a child

I walked

On damp leaves

Under

Dripping tall

Trees

Stretching

Their limbs

To protect

My

Childhood

Dreams

Autumn Stories

Smells

Of autumn

Damp smells

Of smothered

Red and yellow

Telling tales

Of green

Billy Goats

The wind

Against my face

Blows stories in my ear

Unties my scarf

And teases

Me

Into

Belief

The wind I am

You think I am

But underneath

The bridge

I am

A troll

Kicking wooden

Piles in anger

At the insouciance

Of

Billy goats

Yesterday a Cat

Yesterday a cat

With a flat face

Looked out of his

Single window

Blinking softly

The cat

At the window

Welcomed my

Imaginary fingers

At his

Scruffy neck

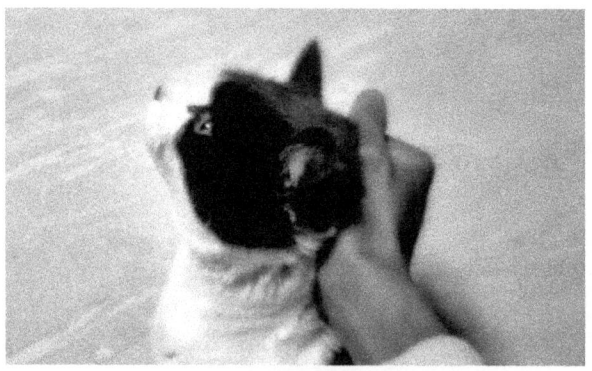

Wild Boar at Five O'clock

I heard the whine

Of wild boar

As they descended

From the hills

At five o'clock

Furry footballs

With hooves

Ready to ravage

Vineyards

Gardens of flowers

And mushrooms

Still hiding

Trembling in anticipation

At their

Ravishing

The Bay Window

The bay window

Sees the dawn

Softly

Watches

The city awake

Hears the garbage truck

Braking

Singing with raspy voice

Gears and hinges

Lifting the detritus

Of the city

To fill its hungry maul

The bay window

Glistens in the newness

Of a city day

Green Parrots Congregate

The San Francisco parrots

Not really parrots*

Congregate in social

Cacophony

Agreeing in loud voices

On a

Common perch

The trees

On Van Ness

Are laden

At four o'clock

With

Green parrots

Not really parrots

Squawking aimlessly

Across

From City Hall

*Actually, cherry-headed conjures and hybrids, still loved as "parrots"

A Tiny Bird

A tiny bird

And then another

Lands softly

To retrieve a crumb

Or two

Underneath the

Table on the balcony

One flies away

Another stays

Pecking for sustenance

To create

Another generation

I watch

My shadow

Holds

And then releases

One small wing

Deep Red Roses

The flowers are spent

Deep red

Flowers of sympathy\

For my mother's

Departure from this life

Deep red like blood

Promising to open

But closed and growing brittle

Curling outer petals

Try to break away

But remain

Curled

Darkening at the edges

Leaves with brown spots

Lie limp

Beneath

Deep red roses

Early Sun

The sun screamed at me this morning

Intolerably bright, intense and loud

Daring me to rise

Reminding me

Of my own impotence

Against her power

I blink

And laugh at her

Yellow arrogance

Trying to break through

The slats of my

Venetian blinds

Or slide between

My eyelashes

Creating cobwebs of bright threads

Pools of colors

Chiaroscuro images

Sliding liquid

Light

A Dog

A dog howls

On Chestnut Street

Which one of our many Chestnut dogs?

There are more dogs than children

In San Francisco

Is it easier to raise a dog

Or a child?

The birds laugh merrily

To hear the dog's howl

The seals at Pier 39

Bark indifferently

The cats

Behind their windows

Bask lazily

In the sun

Soft Twilight

Clouds curl into the evening

Illuminated by fading sun

Hiding behind a blue bed

Wrapped in bird song

Accompanying their own

Bursts of longing swooping

Moving swarms of song and shadow

Billowing and surging in twilight dusk

Flowers close their perfumed petals

Sequestering secrets

Stamen slipping under petals

Butterflies become still

Their delicate glory quiet in the evening

As choruses of color and clouds

Fill the sky with softness

Impossibly Stretched Cat

The cat lies

Impossibly stretched

Curled just inside

Warm rays of sunshine

Finely tracing bits of light

Upon soft fur

His dappled coat

Seems to play games

With dappling shadows

While his whiskers

Twitch

In memory of

A mouse

Wisdom of Life

Can we speak softly and prevail with wisdom?

Flowers blossom every spring

Even creeping up to brighten tiniest cracks in concrete

Thrusting yellow song through sagging gates

Birds sing in the midst of chaos and gritty city streets

Chirping their blessings to the world they see

A world of sunshine and the eaves of roofs

Where they can mate and warm their eggs

Where they can welcome tiny balls of fluff

Feed ravenous beaks

Open wide to all they see above a broken shell

Ready to trust what lies beyond

To trust and expect nourishment and warmth

Surprised perhaps by fog and rain and wind and storms

Yet wise enough in hours to take what nature gives

Living in the moment with the wisdom of all life

Can we not be so wise as flowers and birds

To stretch our roots and see beyond our birth

To greet the earth and sky and sun with trust

Knowing that we are part of all

That seems so new and strange

And learn to fly with wings of wisdom

Speaking softly

Gently carrying pushing striving hoping loving as we must

Something Scary

Eleanor Roosevelt

Told us to do something scary

Every day.

The smaller I am

The scarier the world

As a mouse

I worry about the cat

And as cat

Hide from the dog

But as a bird

I am

Ambivalent

I understand

The scariness

Of every

Day

And sing

Eleanor Roosevelt

Would understand

On the Yangtze

Forty million people in a city by a river called the Yangtze

Rivers intersecting rivers, people intersecting people

History melting history making history

Melting crossroads upon crossroads cutting through beside along

the mighty Yangtze

On the Yangtze

And the moon's sweet slice of lemon rises

As the red sun slides

Behind the mountains

On the Yangtze

Cradling the viscous waters

On the Yangtze

Golden waters, flower tresses undulate in brilliant twilight

As pagodas boats and temples slip aside

And slide beside the flowing Yangtze

On the Yangtze

Shadows of Clouds

Shadows of clouds

Resemble shadows of angels

Bearing watch

Guarding observing leaping with angelic grace over hedges over broods of animals chipmunks scurrying wolves nursing young beneath trees extending prayers green prayers into the blue

Shadows of angels

Resemble sprits of clouds

Blessing earth

Weaving into feathers of birds cameras of drones children playing in puddles in mud among toys of scrap, wooden Popsicle boats and acorn dolls, twiggy hangars and grassy cribs full of lullabies ideas

Shadows of shadows

Light of light

Shining darkness

Speaking singing night and stars bombs and bread death and knowledge murder and birth tears and laughter remembrance forgetting pondering hearts of ages and tomorrow

Shadows of never

Shadows of always

Intending shadows

Attending shadows observing hands raised prayer supplication surrender pleas of hope resignation hands of Jesus hands of Mary

hands of Gandhi of Mother Teresa of Martin King hands of
poverty stretched upward for life stretched upward don't shoot
Shadows of hands
Shadows raised
Shining shadows
Thousands of shadows of hands raised yesterday today Jew
Chinese Buddhist Muslim Christian Hindu Indian Tamil African
child old woman soldier king pauper hands raised don't shoot
Shadows speak
Let this cup pass if it be thy will let this moment see justice see
mercy
Shadows of hands shadows of supplication shadows of prayer
shadows of fathers raising their children to the sky for blessing
Shadows of clouds
Resembling shadows of angels
Bear watch
Pray for us
In this hour of death
Bring life
In this hour of violence
Bring mercy
Shadows of angels
Resembling shadows of clouds
Cover us
In peace

Accepting the Sun

The sun was hard in my eyes this morning
Like a bursting sunflower or an exploding star
The ocean was wet under my feet
Cold and hard
Like nature wanting to be unfriendly
Wanting people to go away
Or be content with walking under sunshine
Walking on sand beaches
Be content without drilling into earth
Drilling into the Gulf of Mexico
Where oil would spill on marine life
On birds that had not been shot at already
By people eating turtle soup
From endangered turtles
Harvested for their shells
Thrown over on shorelines
To struggle on their backs
Until death or slaughter took their souls
The sun was hard
Unyielding and unforgiving
Of its human dependents
Drilling into their mother
Nourished by her rays
Sun and water

Air and land
Ask only to be
As we might be
Laughter dance and song
Upon green and blue and yellow
Sapphire life
Yellow straw
Faded thoughts
Under hot sun
Walking on cold sand
Isolated pleasures
Seeking only being
Allowing the hard sun
To warm and soften her children
Accepting what is
Accepting life
Like coffee in the morning
Accepts you
Draining its cup
And seeks
Nothing

Today the Clouds

Today the Clouds

Today the clouds hung listlessly

Etching gray lace across the horizon

Veiling the sun for moments

As she invited them in for tea

Just to brighten her spirits

Spilling a few drops

From her boiling kettle

Into a sullen sky

Cat's Tail

A cat's tail lies upon the bay horizon

Softly curled above the headlands

Resting under shadowed mountains

Disembodied from its corpus

Dissipating into fragments

Burned off from warmth it craves

Brushing windows in the bay

Curling into sunny spaces

On soft sinking shadow places

Just a tail of foggy softness

Disappearing in the morning

Melting under solar brilliance

Into moving golden waters

Shimmering tail of cool forgetting

Curves and waits a tired sun's setting

Twilight in the Rain

Evening glowed golden red at twilight

While rain fell

There should have been a rainbow

But the sun was indifferent

As she tucked up into dark mists

Bathing the world instead

In colors of reflected fire

Cool fire on a dying Sunday

Streets wet

Windows covered

In crystalline drops

Scattering in the wind

Gossamer sheets of rain

Still brushing naked trees

Blushing in an afterglow

Of a suggested sunset

Hidden beneath

An invisible horizon

Closet Door

The slats in the sliding closet door

Look all the same

Proceeding horizontally across the door

Each succeeding the other

Vertically

Regimentally

And yet through shadows and light

Each reflects different whites and grays

Spots of dust

Scratches

Marks of time

Seemingly changeless

And yet each moment different like each memory

Proceeding from my thoughts

New and old

Never caught in static light or shade

Toned in worry

Colored in regret

Softly lighted with the white of happy moments

Veiled in dust and scarred with gentle remembrance

Willow

Blossoms
Buds
Pussy willows
Emerge from the marsh
Brackish water near ocean shores
In corners and curves
Near beaches and ponds
Adapting
Pushing buds of hard cotton
Above tangled masses of
Lean bending branches
Willowy
Willows
Lean
Resilient
Weeping willows
Drop their tears
Myriad soft threads
Silken brushes
Rustling
Through a world
Of sorrow

Care

Care

Carry

Carrying

A mother a child

Atlas the heavens

We carry each other

We carry our lives

Carry caring

Caretaker

Careless

Digging up of earth

For fuel

Careful

Caring for the earth

Planting gardens

To replenish the earth

Carrying

Harvests

Carrying the world

Sharing burdens

Carrying

Sharing

Care

Buds

The children
Refugee children
Homeless children
Orphan children
Children of the world
Like buds
Sprouting from seeds
Left randomly
By birds or wind
Carried on rivers streams
Floating in ponds
Muddied sullied
Blown aloft
Lost
Ravaged
Anonymous
Tenaciously sending tendrils into the earth
Hanging on to life
As to the sprouting twig
Intrepidly pushing up towards light
Intrepidly pushing
Buds
To open
Into light

Wrinkles

Wrinkles on my hand
Heaving hills cross space
Like hills of earth
Wrinkles of earth
Traversing her history
Her evolution of change
Earthquakes
Water
Hurricanes
Fire
Conspire to form
Rivulets of change
Massive mountains
Valleys
A giant's wrist
A giant's hand
Aged through the years
Into rivers and valleys
We ourselves may view
Or traverse
Hike to their summits
To view sunset or sunrise
Over rivulets
Of earth's own wrinkles

Waiting Clouds

The air is chill

The sun ragged

Clouds are in hiding

Waiting

Winds ruffle the sea

As hands tousling waves

Upon singing currents

Laugh back at

Waiting clouds

Sliding into

Memory

Stripes

Her shirt has horizontal rainbow stripes
The stripes walk up the hill with her
Leaving behind a yellow striped crosswalk
Striped vents on a garage door
Stripes cascading
Intercepting as brick
Bricks on a wall
A wall
Another shirt walks up the street
Vertical stripes
Like the gate to its right
That in turn
Remind me of cages
A beautiful day
My coffee is hot
And I see stripes walking
And I am reminded of
Walls and
Cages

EVE II

A large chest stands down stage center. Stage right is a chair and table on which sits a coffee mug.
Center stage is a large armchair, to be addressed as the throne of the king.
In the chest is a heart shaped box, a pillow, a book, a jump rope, a long t-shirt with a heart painted on the front, a wrap-around skirt (white ball gown type), house scales, tape measure, knife.
Eve enters, stage right, carrying basket of apples.
(option #2 is to enter from back of auditorium, passing out apples)

Eve Scene (Womankind)

An apple is an evil, evil thing
Witches and worms, poisons and germs
Snow White was tempted to chew
Symbol of lust,
Devils and dust
Evil that Eve should eschew!

Adam, quite frankly, was ready to roll
I merely gave him a chance
Now I'm to blame for his lost manly soul,
Just cause he got in my _____

An apple is an evil, evil thing
Witches and worms, poisons and germs
Snow White was tempted to chew
Symbol of lust,
Devils and dust
Evil that Eve should eschew!
I don't much care for the taste of this stuff (sits at chair, takes coffee)
Give me a *café au lait*
I'm not the only one who's had enough
Apples are really passé!

An apple is an evil, evil thing
Witches and worms, poisons and germs
Snow White was tempted to chew
Symbol of lust,
Devils and dust
Evil that Eve should eschew!
 (Goes down stage front)
Women about me, you've something to say!
Stand up for Eve and her choice
I didn't care for the apple that day,
I merely wanted a voice!

(takes basket of apples, carries them to King's chair)
Catch some woe
Catch me on the toe
Carry all these apples to the king!
(sits on chair, with one apple)
Is it curiosity
Or just plain perversity
That made me want to bite into this thing?
(lies back on chair, feet up)
Catch some woe
Catch me on the toe
Carry all these apples to the king!
(Curls into chair)
God or Zeus or Jupiter
Had to call on Lucifer
To question why I questioned why!

Catch some woe
Catch me on the toe
Carry all these apples to the king!
(sits on arm of chair)
And I asked the king
Why was God so mad
When Adam also ate the apple
He should call me bad!

Catch some woe
Catch me on the toe
Carry all these apples to the king!

If bad is asking why
I think I'd rather die
Than say I'd never wonder
And then have to lie

Catch some woe
Catch me on the toe
Carry all these apples to the king!

(Goes down stage, stands at chest)

You made me Eve, Pandora, Psyche as well
Just an excuse for your vision of hell.
Murder and Mayhem
The evil of Eve
You fought all your wars
And you left us to grieve
And sigh
And cry
And ask why--

Catch some woe
Catch me on the toe
Carry all these apples to the king!

It was we who opened the latch of hell's gate
By choosing some fruit
And disarming a mate
Picking the locks
On sweet Pandora's box
To let out
The cries
That ask why--

Catch some woe
Catch me on the toe
Carry all these apples to the king!
(Opens chest, puts on white wrap around skirt, closes chest)

Pandora Scene

Pandora (sings):
Pandora's beautiful
How can that be?
What then is beautiful
If that is me?

They say I'm lovely
Lovelier than a sigh
What then is lovely
If that is I?

God sent the stars to make my hair
Zeus picked bluebells mixed with sky
For my eyes
Lilies and orchids perfume the air
Where I walk
And I talk

They say I'm lovely
Lovelier than the day
They say I'm fairer
Than all the May
Dewdrops and honey make my skin fair
Apollo's rivers wash my soul
All of the breezes teach me to please
And the trees
Teach my body to dance.

They say I'm woman
Woman at her best
If this is all I am

Is this then all I am?
No, there is more I am
Behold the rest!

Pandora is to be adored.
That's why Pandora was made.
So why was I given this box
Where all of the thoughts
Of the gods were laid?

Someone said
It was wrong to look
Someone said
Don't undo the hook
Someone said
You must never
Lift the lid.

But if someone says
That it's wrong to see
Someone says that it's wrong to be
Don't you think
You'd be right if you just did
Lift the lid?
(Opens chest)
Deep in the corners are secrets,
Thoughts that were not to be known.
Dragons and demons and winged things
The devil himself on his throne.
Why did Zeus make those creatures
And give them to me to guard
How could Zeus in his wisdom
Make Pandora the brunt of the bard?
(Takes book out of chest)
Just take a look at these devils
Are they really so bad?
One is called truth, one is called justice
Courage is this little lad.

Here is a box of secrets
That tend to confuse those with guile
They've all been let out
To run, scream and shout
How awful how evil, how vile!

Zeus made me beautiful
And thought me vain
Thank god there's something more
I have a brain!

(Places book on table)

Though I've unlocked all the demons
Scattered the seeds of despair
I have the key to forever
Under my glorious hair

(Pulls up hair, ironic gesture)
They say I'm beautiful
How can they know
That what I've left inside
Is what I've got inside
They call it wondering!
They call it life!
They call it hope…………..!
It's beautiful.

(Goes to King's chair)

Catch some woe
Catch me on the toe
Carry all these apples to the king

I was conceived
To be evil as Eve
But if Eve is so evil
Then let Good deceive

Let Popsicles poison
And dandelions growl
May only weeds sprout
From what was Eden's soil

If Love should prevail
On the far side of Lust
May Eve's apples be weighed
On the side of the Just.

(Takes basket of apples, places them next to throne, stage right. Goes to chest, takes out scales and tape measure, places them next to throne, stage left. Returns to chest, takes off skirt, puts on t-shirt with heart painted on it)

Catch some woe
Catch me on the toe
Carry all these apples to the king!
(Weighs herself on scales; gets off, measures thigh with tape measure)

Psyche scene
Eve asked why, Pandora too
And questions boiled the devils brew
Now as Psyche I must rue
That beauty's deemed a demon too.

Wise we are who chose to question
Yet we still allow deception
Thinking beauty's pale facade
Will make us closer to a god.

Apples make a meager myth
Of plenty fain displaced by pith
Skinny women, skinny thighs
Measure calories and lies

(Gets on scales again)

Catch some woe
Catch me on the toe!
Carry all these apples to the king!

Pithy waists and pithy toes
Scrawny arms and bulbous woes
Just whose body should I borrow
To be lovable tomorrow?

Catch some woe
Catch me on the toe
Carry all these apples to the king!

(Takes scale to place in chest)

Sin and sorrow, love and lust
Kings are born and kings are dust
Prozac is a weary queen
For worn out souls, the golden mean.

Beauty, beauty, beauty is an evil thing
Bottles, apples, compacts, laces
Psyche's soul has many faces

(Breaks off, runs downstage to confide in audience)

Swore I did never to marry
It was Venus made me tarry
Since my beauty made her jealous
She demanded men more zealous
At her altar, at her grail
Found their tribute far too pale.

Catch some woe
Catch me on the toe
Carry all these apples to the king!

Petty were the gods, for surely
Venus bore her envy poorly
Asking Cupid as her son
To make me wed a monstrous one.

Yet my flame smote Cupid too
When Cupid's arrow Cupid drew.

(Takes pillow from chest)

Night and I shared Cupid's bed
No dearer soul could I have wed.

And yet to marry and not see
My love is never married be
And so I lit my husband's bed
To see the man whom I had wed

And cupid woke and fled in fright
When oil dripped from the lantern's light
So I was guilty of disgrace
For gazing on my husband's face.

Foolish Venus, foolish she
Foolish Cupid, foolish we
For a question, for a look
My sweet Cupid me forsook.

Pressed to question, pressed to dare
I was sent to Hades lair
To redeem my Cupid's grace
By gathering charms for Venus' face.

(*places pillow next to chest, gets heart shaped box out of chest*)
Questions, cunning, games and wit
Confusing soul with ass and tit
I stooped once to seek a smile
Wrapped in fine cosmetic guile.

And once I again I disobeyed
And once again Venus dismayed
By looking in the box I bore
To see what beauties lay in store

(Kneels, hugs pillow)

Cupid sent me blessed sleep
Lovers, love and weepers, weep!
Venus, I slipped once I swear
And lost my pride to win your dare

But goddess, as I love your son
I met your challenges each one
And as I faced each passing trial
I saw in heaven Cupid's smile

You had only once to ask
I accepted every task
Though your challenges were vain
I had only love to gain

(Lies on stage, elbows on pillow, facing audience)
How I wept and feared defeat
In separating rye from wheat
Yet ants like Snowwhite's dwarves were mine
To sort the grain in heaps so fine.
Though Jason killed to win his Fleece
I would gather mine in peace.
(Lies on pillow, continues speaking on her back)
Waiting till the trees were full
Of golden fleece and yellow wool.
While sheep came naturally to rub
Sufficient fleece to fill my tub
And when I won though wondering why
I joined my Cupid in the sky
And felt it strange I won with naught
But brains and love and wit and thought. *(Stands, tosses pillow)*

Catch some woe
Catch me on the toe
Carry all these apples to the king!

Heroines will often wonder
What is good in blood and plunder
What a joke, that mortal sin
Could be to question makes me grin!

Questions, questions, core of grace
Give reason to the human race
Questions are the rays of dawn
Though Elsa asked and lost her swan

Asking questions, asking names
Playing coy and playing games.
Shall I know the man I wed
Or take a shadow to my bed?

Ignorance, once Eros' mode
Was neither fair for man nor toad
Shall we always lose our soul
To gain a love, yet pay such toll?

Mystery makes moles of men
Who hide their heads and close their dens
Embrace but half and hush the best
To take a shell into their nest.

Desdemona was doomed to die
When truth was veiled to frame a lie
And Senta lost the Dutchman's grace
When jealousy took wisdom's place.

Gods and goddesses, I pray
Join me as I ask the Day
To let me in the light demand
The truth before I give my hand.

And let us speak and think and pray
To seek the truth of every day
And learn deception is as death
To love or light or soul or breath.

Catch some woe
Catch me on the toe,
Carry all these apples to the king.
(gathers garden tools, hoe, ladder…)
May the seeds of the orchard
Cause beauty to burst
In the warmth of the spring
And the glory of earth

May abundance be prized
And the full bosom's grace
And the hip and the thigh
And a round, laughing face!

Catch some woe
Catch me on the toe
Carry all these apples to the king!

(Leaning on hoe)

God seemed to make of Eve's sweet bite
The Genesis of wrong and right.
So sin was bred in Edens' soil
The progeny of query's toil.

And Psyche and Pandora's wonder
Led to what we dub a "blunder"
Lending thought the fist of yearning
Lifting up the latch of learning.
Catch some woe
Catch me on the toe
Carry all these apples to the king! *(repeats, singing, jumping, carrying hoe off stage)*

Atalanta Scene
(Throws one sneaker, then one sock, then second sneaker, second sock onto stage from stage left)

Atalanta enters in white shorts and top

And I am Atalanta
The bane of my brood
The fastest in Athens
A fate I have rued.

(As she speaks, Atalanta puts on her sneakers and socks)
For as woman I, Atalanta the fleet,
Have seen every victory equal defeat
For even the poets all seem to conspire
To temper my skills with a dose of pure ire.

For my skills Meleager died,
And others, till I learned to lie.
Let me tell you my own story
Lending irony to glory.
(Goes to chest, takes out ivory knife)
I won the hunt
The trophy was earned
His uncles were jealous
Meleager was burned.
Meleager was honest
"It's yours," he said
They turned on Meleager
And now he is dead.
The witches were prophets
Of baseness and hate
Lent a mother a stick
To decide her son's fate.
Mother of Meleager
Listened to the liars
Lit the ember of his soul
And fed it to the fires.

Mother of Meleager
Cruel, cruel day
To avenge your brothers
Your own son you'd slay.
(Places knife back in chest)

Catch some woe
Catch me on the toe,
Carry all these apples to the king.

To punish me for my strong thigh
And nimble foot, I made men die.
What strange and evil world is this
Where skill becomes as poison's kiss?

Meleager's death was not enough
The gods demanded tougher stuff.
So I was made the winner's cup
Where losers drown and winners sup.

When I as woman ran too fast
The gods would stop my feet at last
By slaying heroes not so fleet
To throw their bodies at my feet.

Till I'd weep at all the sorrow
Pray for succor on the morrow
Vow to change the evil mystery
Which would ransom blood for history.

Catch some woe
Catch me on the toe
Carry all these apples to the king!

And Hippomenes as Meleager
Loved me just as true and eager
Though he knew the loser's cost
If I would win, his life was lost.

(Goes to chest, takes out silver dress with three golden apples)

See these apples, golden three.
As we raced he threw to me
And while I saw him pant and sign
I vowed, "This hero shall not die!"

So I paused to gather these
Golden apples on my knees
Hippomenes ran ahead,
And he won the race instead.

Please forgive me womankind
Though I know the race was mine
I chose then to lose my pride
And lose the race to be his bride.

(Takes apples to King's chair)

Catch some woe
Catch me on the toe
Carry all these apples to the king.

(Turns to audience)

Mothers, sisters, daughters, wives
Are we only wombs or hives
Are we the cocoon,
Not the boon of men?

We embrace the human race
Write the text in steel and lace
Choosing life or choosing death
With our hands, our thoughts, our breath.

Catch some woe
Catch me on the toe
Carry all these apples to the king.

(Retrieves basket of apples from King's throne, carries downstage)

Apples, wrap them, seed them, shape them
Color with the blood of mayhem.
For our image from our toil
In our gardens, in our soil

Apples, apples, red and gold
Test the weak and test the bold
Weigh the balance of the scale
Test the truth of Eden's grail.

Questioning, the question's fair.
Why were women not to dare?
Why, for beauty, squeeze their souls
By starving them of worthy goals?

All my apples, take them home.
Feed them to your garden gnome
Let the seed begin to scatter
Through the earth, their pitter-patter.

Catch some woe
Catch me on the toe,
Carry all these apples to the king.

FINALE Eve/Womankind
(Eve walks into audience, sings)

Is this the odyssey of woman?
Are we to bear, to clone, to share
Are we a partner here on terra
To build a world that's just and fair.

Please take my hand my brothers, sisters
My hand is strong, my heart is true
If you will stumble, I'll be steady
And when I fall, you'll be there too.

We make this odyssey together
Accompanying our steps with song
We reach to hold a sweet tomorrow
I'm glad if you will come along.

Let's love and laugh and linger
And take the time to smile
We all can build together
Each stone, each block each mile

We can be good or evil
We can be right or wrong
We need to find a place here
A world for weak and strong

So let's forget the heroes
And let's forget the wars
Just open up your windows
I'll open up my doors.

(Goes back to stage)

Is this the odyssey of woman
Are we to bear our seed alone?
Or shall we share our blessed burden
With those we love and call our own.

(Sits on chair, stage right, sings folk song with ukulele, Watch the West Wind Blow the Grain)

When will we learn that love is here
And life is laughter inside a tear
And there's no reason
To hide our pain
Just watch the west wind blow the grain!

When will we learn that truth is fair
And we are stronger when we share
When will our anger
Lose its pain
Just watch the west wind blow the grain!.

Chorus

Is this the odyssey of woman
Is this an odyssey for man
Are we to share our hopes and visions
Throughout this rich and verdant land.

Is this the odyssey of woman?
Are we to bear, to clone, to share
Are we a partner here on terra
To build a world that's just and fair.

Please take my hand my brothers, sisters
My hand is strong, my heart is true
If you will stumble, I'll be steady
And when I fall, you'll be there too.

We make this odyssey together
Accompanying our steps with song
We reach to hold a sweet tomorrow
I'm glad if you will come along.
I'm glad if you will come along.

Blackout

(Gets into chest, closes chest)

Stage light

(opens chest for curtain call)

AMELIA   (Monologue with song about Amelia Earhart)

Staged monologue with song)

Jan. 11 1935 On Jan. 11, 1935, aviator Amelia Earhart began a trip from Honolulu to Oakland, Calif., becoming the first woman to fly solo across the Pacific

Flute improvises, interchanging with monologue

Amelia is my name
Think of me as a star
Or a vessel in the middle of the universe
Still wanting to soar
Beyond and beyond and beyond
And farther still

Flute

Think of me as a shooting star
That bursts inside its own energy
A wishing star
That wished too much
And still remains
Exploding
In infinite space

Flute

My name is Amelia
A seagull
An eagle
Flying eternally

Flute

Born in Kansas, I see my first airplane in Ohio. I am ten. The airplane? Boring. "rust and wire and wood, and not at all interesting! …I get a peach bas-ket hat at the fair! (sung)

Flute

When my sister and I are little we live with my grandparents.
When I am ten we move to Iowa.
My father is a drunkard who takes us from happy times to poverty and pity.

Flute
Continues with this text:
We leave with our mother for Chicago..

In the First World War I am a nurse. I see men without arms, men without legs, paralized…blind. War is ugly
I must study to become a doctor.
But one day, in California, I fly in an airplane.
That day, I become an airplane. I will never again be locked to the ground.

Flute

I was born in the dawn of the Twentieth Century
It was a century of ventures and mistakes and achievements
I made mistakes
I learned—
I made more mistakes
I yearned
To soar

Flute intermingling with text---flying

I fly 14,000 feet
Higher than any woman has flown
Up in the sky in my yellow bird, The Canary
Far up, a yellow boat to greet the sun

Yellow, yellow
Yellow is bright and golden
Like sunshine and light and hope
And friends and dreams
Yellow
yellow

Flute

I ride a yellow roadster to Boston. The Yellow Peril. Shocking! Shocking!
I help build an airport to make more airplanes. The Boston Globe says I am "one of the best women pilots in the United States".
And I am asked: "would you like to be the first woman to fly across the Atlantic?"
Lady Lindy they say, Like Lindbergh, not cheese, but Charles.
Lady Lindy I am, to follow and fly with the stars
And starlings!

Flute

I meet George Putnam. George. George. George who believes.

We fly from Halifax to South Wales, not Ireland, where we were supposed to land.
I am only a passenger on the journey. But the papers want to make me famous because I am a girl. George puts my name in the papers. George is my friend, maybe more.
I don't know.
George is married.

I fly solo from the Atlantic to the Pacific in 1928.
I lecture. I write. I fly.
I meet with 99 women pilots, the 99's. We cross the states in the Powder Puff Derby. The days are full. I become famous because I am a girl who flies.
George's wife leaves him.
We were only friends

I did not admit that I was in love….
But in February, 1931
We are married.

Flute

And I fly, and fly
Newfoundland to Ireland.
I land in a pasture. Where am I? I ask
A man answers, "in Gallegher's pasture. Have you come far?
From America.
From America

I am the first woman to fly the Atlantic solo.
The French ask, "Can she bake a cake?"
I am all women
I do not bake, I fly.
Baking is perhaps more important.
What I do is nothing more or less
Than being born and living for an idea
One's own idea.

Flute

All women fly in me, all have dreams in me.
1934 Hawaii to California and then to Washington D.C.
Another first for flying.
But I must circle the world for all women.
1937
May, Miami to LA. Then Puerto Rico, Africa, the Red Sea
Onward to India, 22,000 miles.
I am ill.
I am tired.
Dysentery.
New Guinea
June 29th.
7,000 miles to go.
I am tired

So tired.
I cannot hear the reports.
Too many people are talking.
The airwaves are full
I am a celebrity.
I cannot hear the reports.
There is wind over Nukumanu
KHAQQ calling
We must be on you but we cannot see you.

Flute

The gas is running
Low

"George, please know that I am quite aware of the hazards…I want to do it because I want to do it. Women must try to do things as men have tried. When they fail, their failure must be but a challenge to others."
I have already said, I, Amelia, wrote this:
"Courage is the price that life exacts for granting peace
The soul that knows it not, knows no release from little things;
Knows not the livid loneliness of fear,
Nor mountain heights where bitter joy can hear
The sound of wings
How can Life grant us boon of living, compensate
For dull grey ugliness and pregnant hate
Unless we dare the soul's dominion?
Each time we make a choice we pay
With courage to behold the restless day
And count it fair." (By Amelia Earhart)

President Roosevelt sends out nine naval ships and 66 aircraft to search for me but finds no trace.

Amelia is my name
Think of me as a star
Or a vessel in the middle of the universe
Still wanting to soar
Beyond and beyond and beyond
And farther still

Flute

Think of me as a shooting star
That bursts inside its own energy
A wishing star
That wished too much
And still remains
Exploding
In infinite space

Flute
Voice comes in over flute
My name is Amelia
A seagull
An eagle
Flying eternally.

Stage Blackout

If There Were Peace (song with chorus refrain)

If there were peace, the ragged edges of the world would knit themselves together
If there were peace we'd hear the sound of psalms among the clouds, if there were peace
All: If there were peace

Then everyone around the world would look out for each other and each small tear would fill our hearts with pain.
Leader: If there were peace, we'd find a way to heal the world of sorrow, if there were peace, we'd find a way to love
All: repeat

If there were peace, the ocean and the skies above, would soon be filled with music
If there were peace we'd hear such harmony among the clouds if there were peace
All: If there were peace

Then everyone around the world would learn to be forgiving, and each small joy would fill our hearts with hope.
Leader: If there were peace we'd find a way to heal the world of sorrow, if there were peace, we'd find a way to love.
All: Repeat

Until there's peace we'll learn to keep love in our hearts forever and forever and all of us might harmonize beyond the clouds until there's peace
All: until there's peace

When everyone around the world will reach out to each other and offer all our tears and joys in love.
Leader: If there were peace we'd find a way to heal the world of sorrow, if there were peace, we'd find a way to love.
All: Repeat

Leader: And where's there's love, we'll find a way to heal the world of sorrow, where there is love, we'll find a way to peace.
All: Repeat

May All of us Find Love (There once was a woman who lived in a shoe)

Ref.

May all of us find love
May all of us find hope
May all of us find happiness and light
May all of us be kind
May all of us be wise
May all of us remember what is right

There once was a woman who lived in a shoe
Who had many children and knew what to do
She loved them and sent them out into the world
To spread all the love that they had, that they had
To spread all the love that they had.
Ref. may all of us …………..

.
There once was a man who had many things
And one day he gave them away
With each thing he gave he discovered again
He was richer by far in his soul in his soul
He was richer by far in his soul
Ref. May all of us………..

There once was a child who wished on a star
Who wished son a star far above
And when she grew up her wishes came true as she learned every day how to love, how to love, as she learned every day how to love.
Ref. May all of us………..

Song for the Persian New Year (song with drum)

1. Tulips and Hyacinths, red and yellow

Bring me your happiness, sweet and mellow

May sadness depart and the keys to your heart

Bring a new year, a new year of joy

Ref. May Persia be blessed in the New Year with hope and love and joy!

2. Dance in the springtime a year of good news

Let the children find presents from Amoo Norooz

Let us find peace, may all sorrow cease

And Hajii Faruz bring us joy!

Ref. May Persia be blessed in the New Year with hope and love and joy!

3. Fill up a bag of blessings and fun

Play on the tambourine, play on the drum

Dance in the spring, may each magical ring

Bring a cup full of magical joy, of joy; bring a New Year, a new year of joy!

Ref. May Persia be blessed in the New Year with hope and love and joy!

In Persian mythology, King Jamshid was said to have had a magical seven-ringed cup, the Jame-Jam, which was filled with the elixir of immortality and allowed him to see the whole universe

Last Night the Moon

Last night the slender crescent moon

Sailed against the sky

And disappeared

Behind the urban skyline

This morning a tiny cloud

Slid across the horizon

Telling soft stories

She too disappeared

In wind and air

Now at the pier

Paddles are ready and a canoe shoots out into the bay

Against the sunrise

Against blue on blue

Paddles reflect the gold of the first sun

Against a sky of silver blue

Where clouds are re-assembling

Underneath the memories

Of a crescent moon

My Hummingbird

My hummingbird

Yes, she is mine

Swoops quickly in

To kiss my flowering basil

Retreating on her

Tiny

Feathered

Motors

A Hummingbird Spins

A hummingbird spins over rustling leaves

Leaving her joy of flying over leaves

Dying crisply, gently pristinely falling

Emptying the space among the boughs of ornamental pear

For future buds and leafing leaves

She spins

Leaving her joy

To enter brighter sweetness

Autumn Etchings

Autumn etchings illuminate a pristine world

Layered above pain

A man starves for justice in Palestine

You say Israel

Does it matter to the starving man

Hungering for justice?

In Guantanamo another dies in desperation

Perhaps of hunger, perhaps torture

Does it matter to a man cuffed and pinned

Knowing of no charge, no crime,

In solitary confinement for years upon years?

Autumn sings of abundance

Of joy, harvest, and the beauty of dying leaves

In Guantanamo and Palestine

Autumn's dying

Leaves the dead in silent agony of

Unredressed and ultimate

Complaint

Morning Endeavor (September 21)

A Boeing 747 carries the shuttle Endeavor into history

Birds fly under its mighty blast

Nimble messengers of air witness millennia of history

Their own history

That of flight and survival

Evolution from the Jurassic

The feathered theropod

Archaeopterus becoming a squalling crow

Our feathered ancestry challenging us to fly

Sometimes to destroy as malfunctioning angry birds

Learning violence

But also learning to soar way above the stratosphere

Only to return

To the chorus of birds

The song of sweetness

The Moon a Cross

The moon casts shafts of light tonight

As if emulating a cross

If I believed in signs I might call it a vision

Pagan, Greek, Christian? A Celtic cross?

A cross that inspired crusades

Violence, xenophobia, war

Or a silver, shafted moon that inspires love

Romance, marriage, children

Perhaps the shining bars sent out from the moon

Are weather induced

How moondane

But then Don Quixote might ride

These moondane moon bars like windmills

Or challenge them upon his glorious steed

Defy their brilliance

While I below

Receive in joy

Their ineffable

Luminosity

Kwan Yen to Repair

Our little Kwan Yen statue fell last week
And lost her lovely head
Kwan Yen
Spirit of beauty
Spirit of love
Who gave her arms and eyes for her father's life
Only to be blessed with profound remembrance
Remembrance for her beauty and compassion
She waits for glue
Her head upon the dresser
Smiling in genuine humor
Beneath her lovely bending body
I wonder what she might be thinking
Separated from her person, her globe and pedestal
Is she lonely for her arms and feet
That she had once given away in life for love?
Or is she giggling at the humor of the eons
Waiting with her on the dresser
Beneath her disembodied self

Evening Sky and Rapunzel

Orion faces southward in the Eastern sky

Bejeweled with ruby Betelgeuse and sparkling Rigel

Viewing a veiled moon who hides demurely in the moving fog

Brilliantly illuminated then lost in passing clouds

Her veil is flung upward and beyond

Covering the spires of Saints Peter and Paul and

The neighboring Transamerica pyramid

Capturing all but the windows of Lillian Coit's tower

As we imagine a Rapunzel bending over

To fling her hair below

And gaze above her tower

Where the hunter is now hid in fog

Or has vanished

Chasing past

The fall horizon

My Daughter and a Pug

Jesus had a wife perhaps

My daughter has a dog

I was reading about the one

When my daughter called me about the other

I don't know if there is a relationship

But my daughter has a heart as big as the moon

The dog had multiple cancers to be surgically removed

And 16 black teeth to be extracted

When my daughter's eight year old son

Who knew the dog

An old pug

Heard that the dog

The pug he knew

Was to be euthanized

Euphemism for

Yes

We know

The dog's owner had lost him

Perhaps intentionally

The little boy

My grandson

Who knew the dog

And is a little boy

With a big heart

Not a realist

Cried

My daughter knew

She would soon have a dog

A single mom with a job and a little boy

And an old dog with few teeth

Who must eat soft food

And recover from cancer surgery

And sleep in a soft place

And have friends

People around him

Because a little boy could not

Let him die

The world spins in words and stories

Someone wrote that Jesus had a wife

The phone rings

My daughter has a heart

As big as the moon

The Land Suffers

The land suffers

The land a living thing

Screaming from wounds

Of extraction, mining

Pesticides, herbicides

Manipulation of its genome heritage

Invasion of its being

Penetration of its heart

The land is full and real

Flowing with arteries

Recycling in veins of life

Air water earth fire

Animal plant rock

Structures made by flesh

To house and shelter

Stickiness solidness

Asking only to regenerate

Its own pure being

Uncontaminated

Unexploited

Virgin

Singing yearning to embrace

A pure and uncontaminated spirit

Indigenous peoples animals plants

Cry for their home

On plains islands mountains

Streams oceans

They cry for us all

Even for the exploiters

For we know not what we do

We all must scream

That the blood of life may flow again

Pure and holy

Throughout the earth and beyond

Now

And unto the next generations

Life Comes Full Circle

Life comes full circle

And savors the sight and sound

Of sparrows grasping for their feed

Of bugs escaping under crumpled leaves

Of tenderness and children's voices

Laughter floating in the street beyond the trees

Life savors simply being

I am home from the doctor

Little lumps under the breasts

Nothing to worry about

Of course, not to worry like not to think of a white bear

And yet life becomes ineffably real

When there is a precariousness to its neverendingness

For you or those you love or those others love

Or who simply are

A wonder about the fragility of seasons

The grace of simply being

The grace of living with the sparrows and the bugs

And the laughter and the tenderness

Mortal yet forever

Jacqueline Makes Soufflés

Jacqueline makes soufflés

She has made soufflés

For 30 years in North Beach

On Grant Street

Next to the Savoy

Where Dixieland jazz

Echoes down the street

Every Saturday afternoon

And children dance outside the open windows

Jacqueline is ageless like her soufflés

Jacqueline makes soufflés

She speaks to them In French

Telling them to rise

To remain moist

To remain in place

Until their ultimate recipient

Becomes

Their destiny

Chrissy Field, Fleet Week

We are pretending to be homo sapiens

Say the children as they pound rocks on the rubble

Rubble that lines the bay feeding into the ocean

They wait for ships to pass

And Blue Angels to fly overhead

You are homo sapiens, says their mother

You are human

She joins them

Pounding rocks

But we want to be something else

Say the children

As they proceed to split rocks with harder, sharper rocks

A parade of ships passes under the Golden Gate

Battleships evoking past wars

Making waves

Banishing sea creatures, ducks, seagulls, sea lions and pelicans

Eventually the ducks and gulls return

And sea lions

The pelicans fly overhead

Close to the water

Penetrating the blue with their laser eyes

Seeking silver flashes of fish

The children leave their rocks and fantasy

A man in a red shirt, barefoot

Walks by with a guitar strung over his back

A companion strums his banjo

Refugees from the crowds

At Hardly Strictly Bluegrass

In Golden Gate Park

Or simply stray

Musicians

Returning to the bay

After the wake

From the parade of ships

Had finally subsided

Along with vestiges of

Past wars

Coit Tower is a Pumpkin

Coit Tower is a pumpkin

Now in mid-October San Francisco

Dresses for Halloween

Or for the Giants

Coit Tower glows orange

To celebrate baseball in October

How many little boys and girls

Will dress as giants or baseball players

For Halloween?

Ghosts fly through Trader Joes

Tarantulas climb and entangle themselves in cobwebs

Do tarantulas live on cobwebs?

Who decides what color

Coit Tower will sport this evening?

By dawn the blushing orange silo has discarded

Its glowing orange

And stands unperturbed

Upon its hill

Normal

As if it cared

La Jolla Cove

The last step onto the beach is a meter long

I clamber down

Prepare to enter the chill water of the cove

Snorkel and fins and I cast off in tangles of kelp

Hiding orange Garibaldi fish

Darting and lounging in the waters

Among the seagrass and smaller fish

Past the cormorants who scream from piles of rocks

Guarding the dark mouths of caves

Under waves and carven arches I swim among sea lions

Grey and black on their rocky promontories

Silver white as they roll deep in the water

Coming up for air and sociability

Their whiskers skirt the surface

Below their black noses and eyes

Six heads turn towards me

Then disappear

As I too disappear beneath the waters

Gliding towards

Cobbles and sandy shore

October Rain

October rain

Delicate now

As if not sure it wants to welcome winter

Brushes lightly on the window pane

Drips in slow, bright, luminescent streaks

Straight, unslanting in the still and windless afternoon

Then hesitates in slow whispers of wet, stuttered speech

Kissing the window pane gently

In farewell

October sun

Pale and ghostly

Dares to edge itself outside

From behind sodden clouds

Burns itself through foggy skies

Brushes up against the dampened window

Bright warm fingers making tatters of the veil of raindrops

Fragments disappearing back into the vessel

Of October clouds

October Trees

October trees

Still green

Shed dying leaves

Quite subtly

Hiding each dismemberment

With still green foliage

Rustling in conversation

Prideful as if seeking to dissemble

A deciduous destiny

Animated in the wind

Like cheerleaders

With green pompoms

That celebrate victory

And deny defeat

Yet undeniably transformed

By that same animating wind

That turns green shining pompoms

Into crisp and crackling

Remnants

Of retreat

The Voyeurs' Eyes

How quickly banks of clouds

Denying access to the sky

Hiding steeples, telephone poles and mountains

Shrug away their obstinacy

Seduced by blue and sunshine

To bend and join their suitors

As soft, floating pillows

Embracing in the opened heavens

Blue and bright white light

How clearly then

Each steeple, pole, rock, hill and mountain

Bears silent witness to comingling of clouds and sky

Until the dampened heavens

Close against

The voyeurs' eyes

A Universe of Silence

Ineffable darkness purrs against an ululating moon

High tremolos of stars beat rapidly in pulsing rhythmic splendor

Silent to the distant witness

Yet loud in a cacophonic universe

Of grief and exultation

The small earth spins and decorates the sky

Its own sparkling silence conjured into jewels

Of quiet city lights

Somewhere on that sparkling earth

A dark war screams its silent terror

Somewhere a child cries

Mirroring another's laughter

Muted

In a universe

Of silence

Lethal Dragonflies

Three thousand killed by drones in Pakistan alone

A few targeted for illegal assassination

Why?

Operating outside the realm of law

Drones cannot be arbiters of justice

And if they were legal executioners

How justify the deaths of families, civilians, children?

How justify suspended horror

Seeing visible or imagined drones above

Hovering, waiting

Lethal dragonflies poised to strike your child

Your father

Your mother

You

Anytime

How justify the scars in the mind of a child

Growing up with dreams

Screaming dreams

Screaming in the night

Shivering in the day

Fearing any sudden sound

A knock on the door

A call in the night

How learn to trust a world of threatening skies

A world of hatred?

A man crawls out of a small house

A lone survivor

Burning, aching, holding his fractured skull with bloodied hands

No one dares to enter a lonely house bombed by drones

The rescuers are targeted

Remote control assassination upon the return of the dragonfly

No one dares help

No one

Drones are impersonal

Alien executioners

Indiscriminate destroyers of life

Of community

Of peace

Of trust

Of hope

Arbiters of ultimate and absolute injustice

Murdering with impunity

Trophies

The Halloween Parade celebrates the Giants, winners of the World Series

The trophy passes by, eyes riveted to see a trophy

Ephemeral symbol of victory

Lou Seal waves at the crowd

Eyes the trophy

Ephemeral

My trophies are long gone

A majorette twirling atop marble and wood

Winner of the Stockton Memorial Day parade

A Greek urn for debate championship

First place drama trophy

An imitation slab of the Library at Ephesus

First Place Fine Arts award for the municipality

Best Speaker of student body trophy

Winner of a trip to the United Nations

Ephemeral trophies ephemeral victories

Detritus of my own history

No Lou Seal to eye the rags and tags of my past

Fed long ago to a hungry dumpster

Detritus of life and dreams (at the Juan Miro museum in Barcelona)

A bird nests in a lovely hat

Observing an amorous couple

Two chairs stare

One upside down

Glaring at the laughing bird nesting

Evoking dreams of past

Dreams of renewal

As a child I played under the porch

Where daddy long legs joined me

And my dolls and tea set

The long legged spiders

Crawled up my chubby

Four year old legs

My brothers fed me caterpillars

Occasionally

My mother sent me under the table

To come out a new me

Perhaps I must renew myself

Again

I walk through the garden

I walk through the garden

Listening to the words of birds

Singing their ideas to the sun

San Francisco Ferry Building Book Store

Sterile bowls placed upside down from the concrete ceiling

Spill light diffuse, disappearing

Contents illuminated, burned into nothing but visibility

To be a Martyr or Survive

Gertrude Stein translated Petain

And wanted the anti-Semitic words to be read in the USA

Was she serious or just rationalizing to survive in Germany

Do we make friends to survive?

Did Jesus make a mistake accepting the cross?

And Sophocles drinking the hemlock?

Can we avoid speaking truth with impunity

Just to survive?

9,000 Butterflies

Damien Hirst killed 9,000 butterflies

To make a work of art

Locked in windowless rooms at the Tate Modern

Thousands of butterflies succumbed....

To an unnaturally closed environment and

Thoughtless gallery visitors

Long before their time

Damien Hirst

Created once

a pregnant woman

One side beautiful and dignified

The other skeletal and haggard

Portraying truth says Hirst

Which side is truth?

I vote for happiness

Butterflies in the wild

And my own memories

Of pregnant bliss

And children

Delighting in butterflies

A Headache

A headache should be virtual
 Experienced on screen
Not in the head
Turned off at will
Deleted
Cut
Left in cyber space
Left to its virtual cut reality
Left floating
Unpasted
Forgotten
Virtually
No headache
At all

People in Portland

Layered with t-shirts, sweaters, hoodies, jackets

Hats, no hats

Mittens, gloves or not

Gray skies and mist

Rain an everyday expectation

Thoughts of sunshine forgotten

Or sent skyward to nest in banks of clouds

Holding dark currency

Waiting for someone to crack the safe

And send the currents earthward

December 12/12/12

Time and mortality combat silently

Twelve twelve twelve

I will never see again

An enormous crane

Holds two hard-hatted men

Who pluck away at a cable in a box

On an antiquated telephone pole

Small birds flutter by

Wondering when their perch will again be free

It is a long sunny day

The shadows extend themselves

Across blocks across buildings across streets and trees

Coit tower is half in shadow

The enormous crane

Lifts its head like a dinosaur

Above the trees

Smiling at the shadows

Politics and Dreams

Politics can be cruel and inconsistent

Like civil war

Brother and sister

Enter into mortal combat

After a holiday dinner

Friends battle in chambers of law

Or congress

Then shake hands and lunch together

And laugh

Elected officials speak of remedies for

Homelessness

Incarceration of children

Wage inequities

Lack of health care

Lack of justice

Hunger

Crumbling schools

Looking away

As they pass a man

Lying in the street

Or barefoot on the corner

With bleeding feet

I have seen this

And dialed the police for help

Wondering if this is a mistake

Remembering

I have seen the same police

In riot gear

150 strong

Encircling two injured men

Where the Occupy encampment

Had been six hours before

The respondent at 911 saying

No need for an ambulance

The police are handling it

The police are handling it

The police

Who are the police?

Politics can be cruel and inconsistent

Like civil war

We speak of freedom and democracy

As if we represented these ideals

And yet we finance hate war genocide cruelty torture

Masked as mockeries of justice

We let things happen

Or make things happen

Here or across the globe

Where rags of flags continue to fly

As people continue to die

Beneath their ragged flags

Proudly dying for their freedom

Trusting in the justice

Of a future history of hope

Trusting in the justice of a future truth

A future dream

A future free from the politics of inconsistency

The politics of lies

Trusting in the politics

Of new beginnings

Dying

For the politics

Of someone else's

Dreams

Flag in the Rain in July

The rain lies spattered on the window

Gravity pulls only a few drops downward

A flag blows limply on the hill

A Rothko sky

A first glance all one color

Ultimately revealing myriad nuances

Like life itself

Each day opens to the same window

Today a curtain of glowing orange

Spends itself to greys behind the rain

Today the Mayan calendar ends and begins

A new era

Like a new day

Washes all the earth

With hope

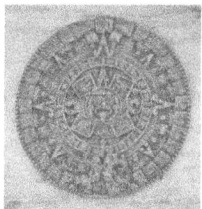

Each day the Sky Dances

Each day the sky dances

To a slightly different melody

The constellations, moons and suns

All throb in a celestial harmony

A mystery of differentiated beats

Each day the sky renews itself

Each day each world and moon and sun

Chants solemnly a variegated running line

Each propagated globus dances onward

To an individuated movement

Bearing witness to a dissonance

Or harmony

Sweetly, wildly, madly, fondly

Bending, stretching, reaching boldly

In the mystery of differentiated beats

Each day the sky

Dances

People Kill

Children die from war weapons

Their protector, the National Rifle Association

Suggests more rifles to more gunmen

To protect schools with armored guards

To create battlegrounds of schools

Like Columbine, which saw its children massacred

And had armored guards

They say to protect children "from bad people with guns",

We need more "good people with guns"

Guns do not kill, people kill

Bombs do not kill, people kill

Three hundred million guns in the United States

Three hundred million means to kill

And we need more guns

More means to kill

More ways to teach our children

The culture of violence

People kill

Yes, people kill with guns

People kill children with guns

Homeless Dilemma

I saw a man stretched out on the street

Close to my home

Not knowing what to do

I asked if he needed a blanket for the cold

He did not answer

The homeless cannot answer

Cannot solve their dilemma alone

The shelters may house victims of tuberculosis

Or offer opportunities for violence

A man may feel safer on the street

The homeless cannot answer

Yes, we need blankets

We need to get through this night

And another and another

And a daytime

When we should seek services

And wait in line

And hope for a shower

And a meal

The homeless cannot answer

We now build homes for the wealthy

Tiny homes, expensive tiny homes

Why not tiny homes in communities

To help solve the dilemma of the homeless

Tiny homes with beds and showers

And a community that reaches out

To bring daytime to the night

And blankets of hope

For the homeless

The Aftermath of Bin Laden

Six nurses were killed and two more murdered fighting polio

Vaccinating children in Pakistan

They were not trusted

Because the CIA faked a vaccination program

To kill Osama Bin Laden

The United Nations has suspended polio vaccinations

Millions of children will not receive vaccinations

Against a pandemic

So the CIA could kill one man

Subverting any claims to legal proceedings

Accessing his home to assassinate

By claiming humanitarian motives

By pretending to extend medical care and protection

Subverting a tradition of humanitarian vaccinations

Subverting a tradition of hope for millions of children

Sandy Struck (October 29, New Jersey)

The moon brought on her highest tides

And lined up with the sun and earth

So Sandy, spurned at Canada's door

Turned, scowling, to the West

Three hundred miles an hour and more

She raced across the sea

Until she piled up on the land

And left catastrophe

At least one hundred

And eleven souls

Were seized by Sandy's might

When she struck on New Jersey's shores

October twenty-ninth

Jesus Born in Palestine

A Palestinian child born in Bethlehem two thousand years ago

Became a catalyst for the slaughter of infants

Who might challenge the throne of King Herod

A catalyst for suspicion that one child might subvert an empire

One child killed is one child too many

One child maimed is one child too many

One child threatened by drones is one child too many

The slaughter of infants betrays humanities deepest instincts

To preserve and protect

The failure to protect our infants

Our failure to protect and nurture

Is a repudiation of life, hope and justice

The life of one child is worth more than an empire

The cry of one new born child

Is worth more than all the weapons known to this earth

Sleep and Children

My grandson didn't want to say goodnight tonight

He is eight- year- old tired

Needing sleep

I think of children on the other side of the world

Not able to sleep

Drafted for war

Or sex

Seven and eight

Eleven, thirteen years old

Not allowed to be children

Not having bedtime stories

Read by their parents or grandparents

Not allowed to escape bombs

Flung by fundamentalist nations

Convinced of their exceptionalism

Convinced of their rights to murder

When it serves their national agenda

Where is it written that children may be incarcerated?

Where is it said that children have no rights?

They do not vote

They have no lobbies

They have only their vulnerable selves

Crying out for protection

In an all too hostile world

I feel the wings of angels

Beating fiercely

Against the wind

The Year has begun

The year has begun again

And the Mayan calendar

Gives us a new start

So much time

Even the present is eternal

Marked in time

And yet

Each moment is a death and resurrection

Each moment our present dies

To be born again

Each new moment

Eternal

Virginal

Do we choose in this moment

A fertile yang and yin

Harmony of opposites

Or do we choose violence again

Choose this moment to shatter our possibilities again

This one eternal present

This Mayan new year or every day

The Common Cold

Must write

Something

My eyes are bleary

Throat sore

Sinuses full

A typical cold

Wanting to be

A metaphor

For anything

If only the distress of nations

Could be as the common cold

Sneeze, blow your nose

Get rest and Vitamin C

And you will be cured

Re-energized

Healed enough

To go on

And be healed, the world

Dark Clouds at Dawn

A large bird stretched itself

Across the skyline

A pelican or blue heron

Huge and yet ephemeral

Encompassing miles of the horizon

Flying into dreamland

Stretching wildly

Like taffy pulled

Over the horizon

Until it disappeared

Pulled and stretched to nothing at all

A large bird looms in my imagination

Pulling me across the world

Around the world

Above the mountains

Flying into nothing

Terror walks the Streets

Terror walks the streets

She who was born in vengeance

Memory her mother

Delivered eternally in loss

Suckled with the blood of fallen angels

Wrapped in sorrow

Rocked in grief

Cradled in steel arms

Of cold and bitter memory

Raised in desecrated

Fields of war's debris

Nurtured with the stories

Of ancestral wrongs

Of holocausts and hatred

Terror is the child who screams for retribution

And finds no solace in the brush of wings

Upon her soft

And yielding cheeks

My Leaf

I saw a leaf just yesterday

All golden with a touch of grey

It vanished when I looked away

So golden for a moment there

Then quickly whisked away somewhere

I wished myself upon that gold

To vanish in the winter cold

All snuggled like a moth inside

I'd swoop and soar and fly and glide

And that is how I'd like to die

Just disappear, my leaf and I

Sublime of Mundane

The Window

A bird taps on the window

Under her tree

It must be her personal tree

Drooping

Darkening the street

Sheltering the window

Bright enough to reflect

Another bird

Or perhaps a real bird

Captive

Behind the panes

Does she need a friend

Or just respite

From sitting

On her nest?

www.ingramcontent.com/pod-product-compliance
Lightning Source LLC
Chambersburg PA
CBHW020922090426
42736CB00010B/1002